NO BOYS ALLOWED!

THE POCKET GUIDE TO

Girl

STUFF

D1053508

To: Amanda

To help you get
through all those
moments that feel
like the end of
the world. —Don't worry
we have all
(Teenage Moments!) had them!

Please know I am
always here if you
need to talk!

xoxo
Love,
Auntie Catherine

NO BOYS ALLOWED!

THE
POCKET GUIDE
TO
Girl
STUFF

BART KING

Illustrations by Jennifer Kalis

GIBBS SMITH
TO ENRICH AND INSPIRE HUMANKIND

Salt Lake City | Charleston | Santa Fe | Santa Barbara

First Edition
13 12 11 10 09   10 9 8 7 6 5 4 3 2 1

Published by
Gibbs Smith
P.O. Box 667
Layton, Utah 84041
Orders: 1.800.835.4993
www.gibbs-smith.com

Designed by Black Eye Design
Printed and bound in Canada
Gibbs Smith books are printed on either recycled,
100% post consumer waste, or FSC certified papers.

Library of Congress Cataloging-in-Publication Data

King, Bart, 1962-
  Pocket guide to girl stuff / Bart King ; illustrations
by Jennifer Kalis. — 1st ed.
     p. cm.
  ISBN-13: 978-1-4236-0573-7
  ISBN-10: 1-4236-0573-X
  1. Teenage girls—Life skills guide—Juvenile literature. 2. Teenage girls—Psychology—Juvenile literature. 3. Teenage girls—Conduct of life—Juvenile
literature. I. Kalis, Jennifer, ill. II. Title.
  HQ798.K517 2009
  646.700835'2—dc22
                                    2008036613

This book makes mention of some activities that could
theoretically carry an element of risk. Readers naturally assume all legal responsibility for their actions.

CONTENTS

★★★

Featuring favorite activities
and cool stuff from
The Big Book of Girl Stuff.

Amanda
For ~~Lynn~~, the best

girl of all.

Introduction

Girls' Introduction!

"FIRST THINGS FIRST, SECOND THINGS NEVER." —*Shirley Conran*

Hello! Take your time with this book. It may be the *best book* you'll ever read. (Of course, the odds against that are pretty high, but you never know! ☺)

We really hope you enjoy it. Now, let's get started!

Adult Introduction!

I may be gender-disenfranchised, but I'm not too proud to beg. And that's why I found myself imploring my five sisters for their assistance with this book. It was a good move; in addition to being loving sisters, they had all coincidentally been girls at one time.

Mary, Sarah, Melinda, Kathleen, and Gretchen were able to provide this project with the little things it needed, like an enlightened outlook, a feminine perspective, and jokes that were actually funny. Our collaboration went so swimmingly, the book's brain trust was then expanded to include other distinguished girls and women.

My collaborators and I hope that readers can find good laughs and even inspiration in the following pages. We've kept a light touch throughout, partly because that's more fun, but also because there is already plenty of high drama in the literature for and about girls today. And while this book contains nontraditional female activities, it also features classic "girl stuff." Why did we do this? Because girls asked us to!

Boys

"OF ALL THE ANIMALS, THE BOY IS THE MOST TROUBLESOME AND THE MOST FASCINATING." —*Apricot Plum*

If boys are the "opposite sex," does that mean that they really are completely different from girls? Let's find out!

Look at the cross-section of a boy's brain. It looks pretty different!

As you go through school, at some point it will seem like all your friends are always talking about boys and couples.

And you'll think, "Everyone's boy crazy! How did things change so fast? We used to dislike boys."

And it's true! If you ask little girls in kindergarten how much they like boys, the girls will rate boys as being "okay." After that, the boys will get steadily worse ratings from the girls every year, all the way through fourth grade. Why do little girls dislike little boys? One theory is that it's because little boys are brats! (What's with all this "cooties" stuff, anyway?)

If ever you find yourself annoyed by a bratty little boy, try using this mystical chant to solve your problem. It was written by wise girls many years ago:

Boys go to Jupiter to get more stupider,

Girls go to college to get more knowledge.

Crisscross, applesauce,

I hate boys!

That just might help you.

Annoying Boy Problems

Here are some other annoying problems that younger boys sometimes have.

ANNOYING PROBLEM: He picks his nose.

IS THIS NORMAL? Yes.

ANNOYING PROBLEM: He likes to give wedgies.

WHY DOES HE DO THIS? Scientists have been studying Boys and the Mystery of the

12

Wedgie for years, and they still have no idea why boys do this. It may be a way primitive people communicate with each other. No one knows for sure. What is certain is that you should keep an eye on any boy who likes to give wedgies.

ANNOYING PROBLEM: He winked at you.

IS THIS NORMAL? The technical term for winking is nictitating. Does that sound normal to you?

ANNOYING PROBLEM: He wrote you this note:

HI!

I'M GUESSING THAT YOU'RE FROM TENNESSEE, BECAUSE YOU'RE THE ONLY "TEN" I SEE! I KNOW YOU'RE GOOD AT SCIENCE. ARE YOU GOING TO BE A FEMALE ASTRONAUT? BECAUSE YOU ARE REALLY OUT OF THIS WORLD! IF I COULD REWRITE THE ALPHABET, I WOULD PUT "U" AND "I" TOGETHER! WHAT DO YOU SAY?

TIMMY

IS THIS NORMAL? Not unless you think it's funny.

As you can see, most boys' problems have to do with maturity. The fact is that most boys mature more slowly than girls. That's mentally and physically!

This is why girls and boys sometimes don't have a lot in common in 6th through 8th grade. (Of course, this is also when many girls get interested in boys.) But boys are *sooo* immature. It makes sense that in many cultures throughout history, girls got married in their early teens, while boys weren't allowed to get married until they were in their 20s or older. This may also explain why so many women end up marrying men who are a few years older than they are.

If you're trying to understand boys, one important thing to know is that a boy never wants to look like a sissy to the *other* boys. That's why even little boys will act macho, like they weigh 300 pounds and are covered in tattoos. It's silly, but a boy starts pretending he's a man when he's just a kid. (And then he never stops pretending for the rest of his life.)

Because of this, as they get older, many boys often won't show much emotion. These older boys are like poker players, but instead of hiding their *cards,* they hide their *feelings.* Your average boy is not going to want to tell you any of his feelings because for him, these are his "secrets."

It's not their fault, though. Boys are often told if they show their feelings that they are "acting like a girl." A boy playing with dolls (or doing any other "girl" activity) is teased much more than a girl playing football (or any other "boy" activity). So life can be tough for boys in ways that girls don't have to worry about.

★ *DID YOU KNOW* that *"MACHO"* actually stands for "Males Acting Childish, Horrible, and Obnoxious"?

★ *"FATHER, MAY I GROW?"* A tribe of people named the Malagasy live in Madagascar. One of their customs is that a boy cannot grow taller than his father without permission. If he wants permission, he must buy the right to grow taller by giving his dad an ox.

Communication

"BOYS FRUSTRATE ME. I HATE ALL THEIR INDIRECT MESSAGES . . . DO YOU LIKE ME OR DON'T YOU? JUST TELL ME SO I CAN GET OVER YOU." —*Kirsten Dunst*

Girls like to talk. That's because it's fun to do something you're good at! There is a scientific reason for this. A girl has shorter vocal cords than a boy, so it actually takes less effort for her to talk. As for boys, their vocal cords double in length during puberty. This can make it a lot of work for them to spit something out! Guys are four times more likely than girls to have a stuttering problem. So, because many boys aren't as good at talking as girls, they do less of it.

★ Studies show the **number one thing guys find annoying** about girls is that they "talk too much."

Boys and their talking problems may not get better anytime soon. Every year, boys spend more and more time playing video games, which isn't very good for their social skills. One of Japan's hottest-selling video games is a "love simulation" game. In it, a boy tries to get a girl to go on a date with him. One young man wrote that he liked the game because he was "not interested in real girls." Scary, huh?

Because many boys aren't the greatest communicators, they often don't understand basic girl language. For example, if you say, "I don't have anything to wear," you *mean* that you're frustrated with all your clothes and none of them look good on you at the moment.

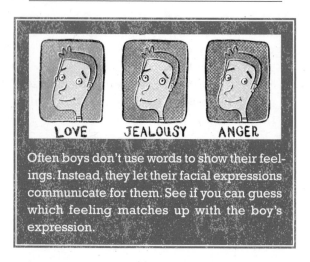

LOVE   JEALOUSY   ANGER

Often boys don't use words to show their feelings. Instead, they let their facial expressions communicate for them. See if you can guess which feeling matches up with the boy's expression.

But when a boy hears you say, "I don't have anything to wear," he thinks you're insane because you have a closet full of clothes. ☺

Guy Fashion

You might be able to tell a little something about a boy from the way he dresses. Many boys just wear whatever combination of T-shirt/shorts/jeans/cap/

jacket that is the guy uniform of the year. Sometimes a boy will even be wearing new clothes, but you'll think they are the same ones from the day before because they look the same. But other guys will branch out more and express themselves with their clothes, shoes, and even hair.

If a boy dresses with style (good or bad), you have to give him points for trying. Let's see what some of the more unusual fashion choices for boys might mean.

Shoes

NONE: Your school allows this?

BIRKENSTOCKS: He cares about the environment!

SANDALS WITH SOCKS: He's either a real rebel or a real nerd . . . or both!

PENNY LOAFERS: Look at the sentence right above this one.

TUBE SOCKS WITH SHORTS: He just got out of a time machine... Retro!

Pants

JEANS: Pretty basic.

KHAKIS: A little more style.

WHITE PANTS: He's probably friendly and he might have ice cream!

LEATHER PANTS: He probably isn't friendly. He probably doesn't have ice cream.

Shirts

TIE-DYED T-SHIRTS: Mean people never wear tie-dye, so he must be nice.

T-SHIRTS WITH ODD OR FUNNY SAYINGS: How funny is it?

MUSCLE SHIRTS OR TANK TOPS: Not a good sign.

SATIN OR SILK SHIRTS: Fancy! He might be a better dresser than most girls.

VELVET SHIRTS: That's REALLY fancy.

VELVEETA SHIRTS: Yech!

Hair

MULLET: If he's plays hockey or is Canadian, it's okay.

SHAVED HEAD: Fine, as long as his scalp doesn't look like oatmeal.

LONG HAIR OR PONYTAIL: If he plays guitar, okay. If he is the Dungeon Master of the D&D club, not so okay.

DREADLOCKS: Cool!

CREW CUT: Classic!

GREASY OR WITH DANDRUFF: Ick! He's shampoo challenged!

FROSTED/HIGHLIGHTED HAIR: He spends more time on his hair than you do.

LOTS OF MOUSSE OR HAIR PRODUCTS: If the fire alarm goes off, avoid him—he could be a fire hazard!

Other

SUSPENDERS: His grandfather helps him dress!

SUSPENDERS WITH A BELT: How hard IS it to keep up his pants?

BOLO TIE: Rodeo star!

BOW TIE: Do you live in North America?

KILT: Now, THIS guy's an individual!

LOTS OF RINGS, CHAINS, OR OTHER JEWELRY: Not a good sign.

A CHAIN ATTACHED TO HIS WALLET: Smart! This stops all those pickpockets at your school!

PIERCED EAR: Fine, but no more than one per ear.

PIERCED FACE: Smile politely and walk away.

PIERCED INTERNAL ORGANS: Smile politely, then RUN away!

TATTOOS: How old is this kid?

Friendship

So far in this chapter, we've done a fair amount of trash-talking about boys. But it's all in good fun! The truth is that boys can be great friends. We're not talking about **boyfriends,** we're talking about **guy** friends. There's a difference.

Guy friends can be easier to hang out with than girls. Even though boys may not be better listeners, you don't have to worry as much about what you say around them. That's partly because the odds are that boys are not necessarily big gossipers. Plus, you probably won't be competing with guy friends, so there's less friction. Finally, guys have their own perspective on life, which means they have interesting ideas you might never have thought about.

Don't let a guy friend assume that being your friend means more than it does, though. A guy might fall madly in love with a girl if he believes the girl is friends with him because she *likes* him. If he goes from *friend*ship to *love*ship, there may be no cure!

Crushes

"YOU SEE AN AWFUL LOT OF SMART GUYS WITH DUMB WOMEN, BUT YOU HARDLY EVER SEE A SMART WOMAN WITH A DUMB GUY." —Erica Jong

Look, this isn't a romance book, but you'll probably have crushes on different people during your life. Crushes are normal, but girls often confuse having a crush with falling in love. You have to be careful.

Do You Like Me?

Mark the correct box:

☐ Yes!

☐ Yes, with all my heart!

☐ Yes, yes, a thousand times yes!

☐ No. I do not like you. *I LOVE YOU!*

Some girls *fall* in love easily, and others just *step in it*. (That is a joke.)

Sometimes a crush can be so powerful that a girl gets completely obsessed with a boy. She can't stop thinking about how great he is and hoping that he feels the same way about her. She gets butterflies in her stomach just thinking about him! Maybe the longest-lasting crushes are the ones we have with celebrities. That's because we (almost) never meet the actual celebrity to find out he's not perfect.

If you ever have a killer crush and want to come back down to Earth, think about this: Almost all women wash their hands after using the restroom. But only 75 percent of men (celebrities included!) do, and the percentage is even lower for boys. Do you really want to hold hands with someone who might not use soap?

If you do have a crush on someone, you might want to keep it to yourself. That's because when other girls find out you like someone, a magical spell is cast and they realize that he's fantastic too! Then they might try to be tricky.

YOU: That Timmy sure is great!

YOUR "FRIEND": Oh, let me tell you, he is SUCH a creep! Let me steer you in the right direction . . . You should be going out with Brandon. He is a great guy!

YOU: Really?

YOUR "FRIEND": You bet! (*To herself:* Now Timmy is mine! All mine! Ha ha ha!)

26

Another classic is when you share that you have a crush on a boy you don't really know. When you find out that your friend likes him too, you feel jealous and possessive, even though he's a stranger!

Finally, this can happen when you tell your friend who you have a crush on:

YOU: That Timmy sure is great!

YOUR FRIENDS (ALL TOGETHER): Ew! He is SO nerdy!

YOU: Just kidding, heh heh.

Your Magic Song

If there's a special someone you like, have a magic song that the two of you share. To find it, get out a picture of your someone. This may be in the school yearbook or a magazine. (The beauty of this spell is that the other person doesn't have to know about it!) You also need a radio, or maybe an iPod set for "shuffle."

Hold the picture and look into your love's dreamy eyes. Murmur his name 5 times. Then turn on the radio (or hit "play" on the iPod.) Whatever song comes on is *your* song together! You must now learn all the words to it, and anytime you hear this song in the future, it will remind you of your special someone.

Are You a Good Match?

Are you wondering if you would get along with the boy you like? Lesley Ann Dunking has a system called Love Letters that can help answer this question. (Keep in mind that this is just a game, okay?)

First, write down your first and last name. Below them, write the first and last name of the boy you like. (This has to do with the letters in your name, which you can learn more about on pages 150–157.) Here's an example:

SUMMER WHEATLY

PEDRO SANCHEZ

Now go letter-by-letter through your name. Look at each letter in your name to see if the same letter is in the boy's name. If the letter IS also in his name, you cross off that letter in both your name and the boy's name. Keep a running total of the letters you have in common. If a letter isn't in his name, just keep going with no score.

SUMMER WHEATLY

PEDRO SANCHEZ

In the example, the "S" in Summer would be crossed off, because "Sanchez" also has an "S."

~~S~~UMMER WHEATLY

PEDRO ~~S~~ANCHEZ

Although the next three letters in Summer have no match with Pedro Sanchez, the last two letters ("e" and "r") do. As you can see in the example above, the tally is three after finishing with Summer's first name.

Now do the last name. Here's what the names would look like when you're done, using this example:

~~S~~UMME~~R~~ WHEATLY

PEDRO ~~SANCHE~~Z

SCORING: There are a total of five matched letters between the two people in our example. Let's see how you score your names.

2 OR LESS: There is no hope of a relationship between you.

3 TO 4: You might have something, but it probably won't last long.

5 TO 6: The prospects are good!

7 OR MORE: True love!

Common Questions Girls Ask about Boys

Q: HOW DO I GET A BOY'S ATTENTION?

A: An easy way to get a boy's attention is to ask for his advice or opinion about something. Boys love to give girls advice on stuff. Compliments work, but don't overdo it.

Q: DO BOYS PAY MORE ATTENTION TO PRETTY GIRLS?

A: What is "pretty" anyway? Haven't you read the **"Beauty"** chapter in this book?

But still, for most boys, the answer to this question is probably "yes." And guess what? The girl who's prettiest in 7th grade may not be the prettiest in high school, or college, or real life after that. *Anyone* could be the prettiest girl then!

Q: *I KNOW A BOY WHO ONLY PAYS ATTENTION TO BLONDE GIRLS (OR GIRLS WHO PLAY SPORTS, OR . . .) WHY DOES HE DO THAT?*

A: Boys are just as insecure about peer pressure as girls are. A guy may feel he *should* like a certain type of girl. The boy might avoid a girl he *actually* likes, because there is another girl he is *supposed* to like. (BTW, girls are just as bad about this!)

Q: *HOW DOES FLIRTING WORK?*

A: The simplest and least embarrassing way to flirt is just to make eye contact with that special someone. Then *hold the look* for around two seconds. (That's an eternity in flirt time!) Going too much longer turns it into a staring contest, which is sort of weird and NOT flirting anymore. While you're making eye contact, smile. Then look away.

That's flirting!

Q: HOW CAN I TELL IF A BOY HAS A CRUSH ON ME?

A: If someone has a crush on you, it's like having your own *fan club*. Somebody out there loves to hear news about you and thinks you're great! We divide boy crushes into two types:

THE SHY CRUSH: This boy gets embarrassed if you even look at him. If you talk to him, he will stammer. But you notice that he stares at you a lot. He's either really shy or he just can't believe (or won't admit!) that he has a crush on you. And yet he will defend you to other people.

OUTGOING CRUSH: This is a much easier crush to see coming. This boy seeks you out and always has an excuse to talk to you. In short, he couldn't be more obvious!

Q: I KNOW THIS IS OFF THE TOPIC, BUT DO BOYS EVER WALK DOWN THE HALLWAY JUDGING EACH OTHER'S HAIRDOS?

A: No. Boys are so different from girls. For example, boys see male fashion models all the time, but most boys don't want to *be* male fashion models. What's wrong with them?

Q: HOW DO I TELL A BOY I LIKE HIM?

A: Don't play mind games. Try being friendly to a boy you like when you see him WITHOUT paying *too much* attention to him. Don't call him constantly. Resist the impulse to hang out together ALL THE TIME. Hold something back. That's because if he *knows* that you have a crush on him, then he is in the driver's seat. And he's probably a bad driver!

Q: I'M SMART AND I GET GOOD GRADES. THERE'S A GUY WHO I THINK LIKES ME, BUT HE ALSO SEEMS TO AVOID ME. WHAT DOES THAT MEAN?

A: He might be scared of you. Evidence suggests that some boys (and men) avoid smart, successful girls. This is because guys are competitive, so they think they have to be the smart ones. If a girl is smart, a guy might think he is "losing."

Believe it or not, research seems to show that the higher an adult woman's I.Q., the more some men will be afraid of her. But as the world changes, smart girls are being seen as leaders and role models more and more each year. So PLEASE don't act dumb so a guy will like you. If a boy can't accept that a girl can be intelligent, you really don't want to be around him anyway.

Q: SO THAT'S IT? HE'S AFRAID OF ME?

A: He might be naturally shy. Or maybe he actually doesn't like you. (Wait, that's impossible! You're adorable!)

Q: WHEN SHOULD I GIVE UP ON A GUY?

A: You can't talk someone into liking you. Nobody can explain these things; we just have to learn to live with them. So give a boy a couple of chances to get to know you. If he's not interested, move on. You will just seem needy if you keep trying after that.

Q: HE REJECTED ME! I AM SO HURT AND MAD. CAN I DESTROY HIM?

A: Getting rejected can make anyone angry, disappointed, embarrassed, or all three. You want him to explain *why* he doesn't like you, or to just give you **one** more chance, or maybe you want sweet revenge on that jerk! Who does he think he is?

You may have these reactions, but remember: He's not your *enemy,* he's just a guy who doesn't want to go out with you. And you're going to have to do the same exact thing to other boys in your life, and that won't make you a bad person either. It's just the way it is!

Relationships

"I DON'T UNDERSTAND IT WHEN PEOPLE SAY, 'WE'RE GOING OUT.' WHAT DOES THAT MEAN? YOU'RE NOT GOING ANYWHERE." —*Tori Allen*

Hey, you're too *young* to have a boyfriend! (If you're over the age of 30, ignore that statement.) So if you don't have a boyfriend—good for you. Who needs 'em?!

Things a Guy Will Never Say!

"DO I LOOK GOOD IN THIS?"

"EVERYBODY DANCE!"

"AM I YOUR BEST FRIEND?"

"DO THESE PANTS MAKE ME LOOK FAT?"

"WHY DIDN'T YOU GET ME A PRESENT?"

But if you **do** have a boyfriend, don't talk about him too much to your girlfriends, **especially** if they don't have boyfriends. It might seem like bragging, and then you'll have relationship problems with the people who really matter: ***Your girlfriends!*** You might only go out with a boy for a day, so if you burn your bridges with your girlfriends, you had better be a good bridge builder when the day is over. ☺

As for boys, remember that they are as sensitive or *more* sensitive than you and your girlfriends. Although they may *act* like they have no emotions, it is just an act. They can (and do) get their feelings hurt, but most boys will never admit it.

If you and a boy like each other, keep it private. That way you don't have to talk to *everyone* about it! If the two of you can make it past the initial newsflash of being an "item," you move into *hanging out together.* Even though this is usually more public, you should avoid PDA (Public Displays of Affection). Good couples don't show off!

Maybe at some point he will ask you a question that is some version of "Will you be my girlfriend?" We don't know what kind of rules your family has about this kind of thing, so use your common sense. If you do decide to officially become someone's girlfriend, at this point a lot of younger boys will enter the *protective/ jealous* stage. You know you've reached that stage if he wants to hang out with you constantly and is jealous of everyone you talk to. Try to stay in groups as much as possible so that it doesn't get weird, and hope he grows out of it.

BTW, don't go out with the boyfriend (or former boyfriend) of one of your girl-

You

HeR
BoYFRiEnd

YouR
FRiEnd

friends. This is almost always a disaster. If something goes wrong (and it will!), you are ruining six relationships by doing this!

Kissing

"WHY RUIN A GOOD FRIENDSHIP WITH A KISS?" —Paige Lundy

In a perfect world, people who share a kiss are sharing a feeling and showing how much they trust and like the other person. The average woman will spend about two weeks of her life kissing people. As for you, you're still a *girl,* so stick with holding hands!

Types of Kisses

The following information is amazing, insightful, and informative! (But remember, you're too young to be kissing anyone.)

THE ESKIMO KISS

The *ESKIMO KISS* is practiced by the Inuit people of the Pacific Northwest. Two people who like each other gently rub

40

noses as a sign of affection. Some people think they do this because their lips would freeze together if they lip-kissed. (And this may not be as silly as it sounds!)

THE CHEEK KISS

CHEEK KISSING is common in North and Central America and the Mid-East as a greeting to a friend or relative. Usually it's one kiss to the cheek (sometimes with a hug), and you're done. In countries like Colombia and Bolivia, a person *always* kisses *everyone* present when arriving or leaving a party or dinner. When you go to a party, you kiss everyone. It doesn't matter if you know them or not, nobody's cheek is a stranger to your lips!

In Italy, Spain, and Holland, there may be two (or three) kisses to the cheeks to greet a person. But the French win for most total kisses: As a gesture of respect, leaders in France sometimes get *four* kisses to the cheeks!

★ *THE KISS OF DEATH!* In the 1500s, it was a crime to be caught kissing in Naples, Italy. The punishment? ***Death!***

THE AIR KISS

The *AIR KISS* is a fake cheek kiss. This is where you get within an inch or so of the person and then "kiss the air" instead of their cheek. This is done as a joke with friends and as an emergency kiss with someone that has dirty cheeks.

★ *MISTLETOE!* For a poisonous plant whose name means ***"dung twig,"*** the mistletoe has a pretty romantic reputation.

FRENCH KISSING

You may have heard of *FRENCH KISSING*. It is also known as ***snogging, soul kissing,*** and ***tonsil hockey.*** The term "French kiss" was invented in 1923, and is not used in France. One reason the French are linked with kissing has to do with a ritual they had 1500 years ago, where a dance between partners would end with a kiss.

Kissing Facts

Most people turn their heads somewhat to the side when moving in for a kiss. They do this because knocking noggins or banging teeth together does not set the mood correctly.

★ *RESEARCH SHOWS THAT 66 PERCENT OF KISSERS TURN THEIR HEAD TO THE RIGHT.*

Kissing around the World!

Not everyone kisses. In Japan, people do not usually kiss in public. And the Chinese were supposedly horrified when they first saw Europeans kissing! It also appears possible that some Native Americans didn't even know what kissing was until sailors brought the practice from Europe during the 1500s.

People with braces have to be careful not to hurt each other when kissing. There are horror stories of brace-faces locking into place and having to dial 911 to be separated.

Ever wonder how "X" came to mean a kiss? (Pretend that you have wondered this.) Well, back in the days before most people could read or write, if a girl had to sign a legal document, she would put down a big "X" for her name. Then to make it more official, she would *kiss* her signature. And even though most people can write now, the tradition of kisses and Xs just sort of stuck around.

If you're not sure yet about your future career, think about becoming a *Kiss Mixer.* That's the person at Hershey's who puts together the ingredients for their candy Kisses. Then if someone ever asks you for a *hug,* you can tell him that that's not your department!

★ *FUN WORD! NIGGLYWIGGLY:* The little paper tag that comes out of the top of a Hershey's kiss.

Hugs

So what about hugs? Well, at some point in every middle school, girl groups go through a "hug phase." This usually continues well into high school. It is when girls, or groups of girls, get the *hug bug*. Girls are suddenly hugging each other

in the hallway all the time, to greet each other, or provide support. While girls in other countries have long been affectionate with hugs, this is still pretty new to U.S. schools.

HUGS ROCK! In the words of one girl, "they are jolly and mood boosting." Two-armed hugs with the heads side-by-side are the most affectionate hugs. The one-armed hug is the least personal. This is when a girl is next to her "huggee" and puts one arm around his shoulders and pulls in. The most personal hug is the Oreo hug, where two people hug a person in between them.

Fights!

There's no avoiding arguments. Sooner or later, every couple has them. Who knows what it will be about? Maybe he thinks that vanilla is better than chocolate (the fool!), or maybe he is trying to get you to do *his* homework. Whatever.

You'll have to work through these things yourself. We think that most fights are really about communication problems, and guys just aren't the best communicators. Remember that just because a boy *likes* you doesn't mean he *understands* you! And remember, these fights are *not* the end of the world. Both of you will get over it.

If you are in the right, the good part about a fight is that he will apologize and maybe even get a gift to make up with you. Happy endings with presents are good! If you are in the wrong (hard to imagine, but still), you will apologize and maybe even give him a gift to make up with you. (Don't give him a gift of makeup, though. He won't think it's funny.)

Breaking Up

> *"ONLY TIME CAN HEAL YOUR BROKEN HEART, JUST AS ONLY TIME CAN HEAL HIS BROKEN ARMS AND LEGS."*
> — *Miss Piggy*

Hey, unless you're getting married, breaking up has to happen eventually. According to our statistics, 100 percent of breakups happen after a couple has already been going out. There are times when the two people decide together that breaking up is the best idea and they are both happy with the decision. (Of course, we've never actually *seen* this happen . . .)

But if *you* need to break up with *him,* there's almost never a good way to do it. There are **BAD** ways to break up, though.

The Bottom Three Worst Ways to Break Up

3. ON THE PHONE OR ONLINE.

2. HAVING A FRIEND TELL HIM.

1. JUST IGNORING HIM AND HOPING HE GETS THE HINT.

You really need to tell him in person and in private. School is a bad place for this, but it will do in a pinch. Try to keep a time limit on the conversation so that you can say your part, he can respond, and you can leave him alone to process it.

Breaking up always sucks, but it's even worse if *he* breaks up with *you.* Many girls get a bad case of **breakup-rexia** after breaking up, especially if it's the first time it's happened. Girls suffering from this illness lose their appetites and don't want to talk much. If you ever get **breakup-rexia,** you will notice that every sad song you hear seems to have

49

been written just for you. Fun things don't seem so fun anymore. Friends and family can't seem to help. But guess what? There is a cure for **breakup-rexia!** The one surefire cure for it is *time*. (Chocolate also helps.) Yep, if you give anything enough time, it will get better. It always does.

Marriage

MARRIAGE?! Hey, slow down there! You should stay single and independent for another decade or so. But still, a girl can't help but think what it would be like if she were married to her special someone . . . even if he is only eleven!

Here's an amazing marriage fact: Adult men and women are usually attracted to people who are like **they** are. Have you ever noticed married couples who look like each other? Believe it or not, the odds are that married couples will have the same kind of nose and the same distance between their eyes. (If you haven't noticed this before, start taking a look.)

★ *A WOMAN'S ODDS* of marrying a million-aire are 215 to 1. A woman's odds of ***becoming*** a millionaire are about 215 to 1. (Go for the second option. That way, the money will all be yours!)

Research also shows that married couples are usually alike with their education, race, religion, politics, and attitudes toward life. Think about your parents. Does this apply to them?

Speaking of your parents, until about two hundred years ago, most girls married someone who their parents picked out for them. Even today, this sort of "arranged marriage" is common in some parts of the world, like India. An arranged marriage is not the same thing as a ***forced*** marriage. Either the young man or woman can call off an arranged marriage if they want.

Do arranged marriages work? Well, the United States has a divorce rate of about 50 percent; in other words, about half of all marriages end in divorce. (The state with the lowest divorce rate is Massachusetts, while the state with by far the highest divorce rate is Nevada.) In India, the divorce rate is currently less than 2 percent. Interesting!

Our Favorite Proposal Story!

An Illinois man named Bob decided to propose to his girlfriend, Teri, by renting a billboard. He had his marriage proposal printed on it:

TERI, PLEASE MARRY ME! LOVE, BOB.

Then he waited for Teri to drive past it.

GOOD NEWS: Teri saw the message and said "yes."

BAD NEWS: Ten other women named Teri who were also dating men named Bob saw the same billboard! This led to eleven relationship problems. (That's because one of those women was dating **TWO** men named Bob!)

Friends,
CLIQUES, SECRETS, AND GOSSIP

*"MANY FRIENDS WILL WALK IN AND OUT
OF YOUR LIFE. BUT ONLY TRUE FRIENDS
WILL LEAVE FOOTPRINTS IN YOUR HEART."*
— *Eleanor Roosevelt*

A good friend is one of the best things
that life has to offer . . . just think,
without one, you'd have to walk every-
where alone! To have somebody you can
be yourself around is a great gift. You can
both say what you really think, because

you're comfortable with each other. Also, a recent study suggests that having close friends leads to a longer life. That's simply perfect. This means that "lifelong friend-ships" just got longer!

The Compliment Kit

"ALWAYS ACCEPT ALL COMPLIMENTS. IGNORE ANY OTHER REMARKS." —Kay Oss

Different friends talk and communicate in different ways. Some girls like to talk so much, they would make good talk show hosts (as long as there were no guests to interrupt them). Other girls use so few words, you might think they are giving you the "silent treatment." But there is one category of words that ALL friends like to hear. *Compliments!*

The cool thing about compliments is that they are *free.* It doesn't cost you anything to make a friend feel good about herself. So if you have a friend who seems down,

try cheering her up with the amazing Compliment Kit! To use it, just combine two of the adjectives from columns *ONE* and *TWO* with a noun from column *THREE* to create a compliment that will make your friend feel great!

ONE	TWO	THREE
gorgeous	witty	queen
smart	fabulous	genius
elegant	friendly	cutie
creative	sweet	duchess
adorable	confident	empress
thoughtful	sparkly	optimist
generous	loving	goddess
striking	responsible	trendsetter
capable	ingenious	princess
fashionable	amazing	diva[1]
wonderful	fantastic	original
magnificent	adorable	countess
shiny	happy	person
fascinating	graceful	lady
svelte	stunning	monarch
saucy	lovely	leader
intelligent	insightful	highness
funny	honest	sister*
open-minded	positive	chica
interesting	pretty	woman
dependable	breathtaking	viscountess
humorous	foxy	pioneer
caring	artistic	czarina**

(*pronounced *"sistah"*)

(**pronounced *zar-een-uh*)

★ ***Complimentary Information!*** Girls give way more compliments than boys. Also, girls make their compliments personal, for example, **"I love your hair."** Boys tend to be more generic: "Nice shot."

Over 60 percent of all compliments have to do with a person's appearance.

And according to the *Oxford Dictionary of English* there are only about forty one-word compliments in the English language.

"SHARED JOY IS DOUBLE JOY. SHARED SORROW IS HALF SORROW."
—*Swedish Proverb*

---

1. *One meaning of "diva" is "a glamorous, admired woman."*
(Another meaning is "a horribly spoiled woman," but that's
not the one we mean!)

Friend Test

Answer the following multiple-choice questions about one of your friends.

1. YOUR FRIEND SAYS SHE WILL BE READY IN A MINUTE. THIS MEANS:

a. She will be ready in sixty seconds.
b. She will be ready in five minutes.
c. She will be ready in about an hour. Go get a bite to eat and come back.
d. You will never see her again.

2. YOU SUGGEST TO YOUR FRIEND THAT YOU GO TO THE MALL. YOUR FRIEND WANTS TO:

a. Do some volunteer community service instead.
b. Go to the mall to see the latest fashions at the clothing stores.
c. Look at guys in the mall's food court.

d. Visit the most expensive store in the mall, because they have the best stuff to shoplift.

3. *YOUR FRIEND HAS A RIP IN HER JEANS THAT YOU POINT OUT TO HER. YOUR FRIEND:*

a. Laughs and either sews up the rip herself, or ignores it.
b. Is surprised and then a little sad as she donates the jeans to charity.
c. Immediately throws the jeans out and goes shopping for a new pair.
d. Says, "I know. I put it there." Then she shows you the switchblade that she cut the jeans with.

4. *YOU HAD A REALLY BAD DAY, AND AS YOU'RE TALKING TO YOUR FRIEND ABOUT IT ON THE PHONE, YOU START TO CRY. YOUR FRIEND:*

a. Tells you she's coming over with ice cream.

b. Tells you that everything will be okay, and that you're wonderful.

c. Says, "Hang on *one* second, I have another call coming through."

d. Says, "Get over it!" and then starts eating potato chips really loudly.

5. *YOU'RE AT A MOVIE THEATER AND YOUR FRIEND NEEDS TO USE THE RESTROOM BEFORE THE FILM STARTS. WHAT DOES YOUR FRIEND DO?*

a. She goes to the restroom.

b. She asks you to come with her to the restroom.

c. She holds it for the whole movie because she doesn't use public restrooms.

d. She asks all 12 girls in the group to come with her.

6. *YOU ASK YOUR FRIEND WHAT THE MOST IMPORTANT PART OF BEING A FRIEND IS. SHE SAYS:*

a. "Loyalty and support."
b. "Enjoying good laughs together."
c. "Forgiving my friends when they let me down."
d. "Sorry, I wasn't listening. Hey, can I borrow five dollars?"

7. *A SHY GIRL WALKS BY. YOU'VE NOTICED SHE ALWAYS SITS BY HERSELF AT THE CAFETERIA AND DOESN'T HAVE ANYONE TO HANG OUT WITH ON FIELD TRIPS. YOU THINK THAT IT MIGHT BE COOL TO GO TALK TO HER AND GET TO KNOW HER A LITTLE BETTER, AND YOU SUGGEST THIS TO YOUR FRIEND. YOUR FRIEND SAYS:*

a. "Oh my gosh, you read my mind. Let's go!"
b. "Her? Really? Okay, if you think it's a good idea."
c. "Funny joke. She is *SUCH* a freak."
d. "I see your plan. We'll pretend to be her friends and then take her lunch money!"

★ *SCORING* ★

a = 1 point   c = 3 points
b = 2 points   d = 4 points

SCORE TOTALS

1–8

She may be *your* friend, but she is *our*
hero! She's either a great role model for
you or it's impossible to live up to her
standards. Or both!

9–16

Your friend sounds like an easygoing,
good-hearted person. Stick with her.

17–24

Your friend really needs you. (She needs
you to teach her to be less selfish.)

25–28

Put down this book and call the police.

Secret Friend Greetings

You see your friend or maybe someone who's on your soccer team walking toward you in the hallway at school. You both smile, exchange your secret handshake, and keep on walking. How cool is that?

Handshakes and greetings vary from place to place. In Central and South America and southern Europe, a handshake can last a long time, and while people shake, they often use their other hand to touch their friend's shoulder or arm. In many Asian countries, handshakes are gentle and there is no eye contact.

Get a secret handshake to share with your crowd or group of friends. Whatever combination of finger wiggles and hand jive you come up with is up to you. We're sure you already know classics like the Soul Shake, the Pinky-Swear Shake, and the Moldavian Friendship Grip. Here are a few other ideas to get you started.

SALAAM GREETING: In many Arab countries, people touch their right hand to their chest, lips, and forehead. This ends with the hand raised (palm out) and a head bow. Extra credit for saying "Salaam" (which is a pledge of devoted friendship).

TIGER CLAW HANDSHAKE: Hold your hand out at eye level with the fingers outstretched like claws. Your friend does the same, and you come together and clasp hands up high.

THE HEART PUMP HANDSHAKE: Shake hands however you want to, but don't release! Give a slow squeeze, relax, give a slow squeeze, relax.

APACHE HANDSHAKE: Reach for your friend's hand like a regular handshake and then keep going and grab them just behind the wrist, while she does the same to you. (This handshake was also a favorite with Roman gladiators.)

NAMASTE GREETING: In India and Thailand, a friend is greeted by putting the hands

together (like you're praying) and following that with a slight bow.

Handshaking experts agree that the perfect way to end a Secret Handshake is with a quick hug. How sweet!

Friendship Bracelets

These are a great way to make the ties of friendship stronger.

YOU WILL NEED: scissors, tape, ruler or measuring tape. For the bracelet threads, you can use twine, hemp, embroidery thread or floss. *Optional:* Beads (with big holes).

First, this doesn't *have* to be a wrist bracelet. It can be for an ankle, or it can be

65

attached to a key chain or used as a choker. For our example, we'll assume you're using hemp or some nice, colored twine.

Measure out your twine according to what you want to make. We suggest that you cut two pieces that are 2 feet long and two pieces that are 1 foot long.

We are going to describe a pattern using four strings. Tie a regular plain knot about an inch from the ends of all four of your pieces. Then tape down the ends of all of them.

So the ends of these pieces are now taped to each other on a worktable. Have the two short strands in the middle, with the two *longer* strands on the outsides.

Throughout the process, you will keep the middle strands tight and straight. Only the outside ones will be moving around. To begin, cross your long left strand over the middle strands and under the right strand. Then take the right strand and

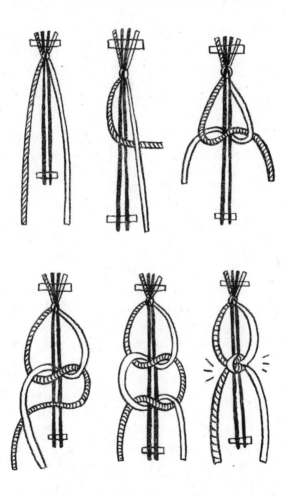

pass it under the middle strands and over and through the first (far left) strand. Tighten it! If you tighten the same tightness each time, the bracelet will come out better.

Then repeat the process for the left strand (over the middle and under the far right strand) but this time after you go under the right strand, form a loop. That way, when the right strand comes back under the middle strands, it can just go *through* the loop that you created.

Tighten it!

If you have any beads, just slide them up the middle strands (which is why the beads need big holes) and keep working around them. When the piece is long enough, you can braid or knot the ends together. Or you can make a loop at the end, stick a bead on it, and tie it off. Or you can tie the ends into a knot right onto your friend's wrist or ankle, which would be the best friendship bracelet of all!

★ Do not give in to the dark side and make someone an "enemy bracelet." ☺

Girl Types

**HELEN: EVERYONE'S SPECIAL, DASH.
DASH: THAT'S JUST ANOTHER WAY OF
SAYING NO ONE IS.** —from *The Incredibles*

Everyone IS special, just like everyone else! Oh well. No matter how unique we are, sometimes we fall into the same categories as other people. The following categories are *just for fun;* check out the girl types below and see if you recognize anyone you know! (And remember, nobody is as clear-cut as a "type" when you get to know them. People are more complicated than that!)

The Nurturing Friend

The super-hero of friends! The nurturing friend is always prepared to help.

ATTITUDE: Terrific! She's there to help, and she makes the world a better place. If you need someone to walk you to the bathroom because you're crying, she's there. Need some advice? Candy? Clothes? Help with homework? She's got you covered.

ACCESSORIES: A heart of gold. (Wait, you can't see that!) A big purse or backpack that contains snacks, gum, makeup, pens with cool colors, safety pins, change . . . whatever you need to borrow.

NICKNAMES: Old Faithful, Best Pal, the Helper.

TRADEMARK LINES: "Call anytime!" "It'll be okay!" "Can I do anything to help?"

INTERESTING FACT: Because she is always taking care of others, the Nurturing Friend may ignore her own needs. Don't take advantage of her good nature, and help her out when you can.

The Frienemy

The Frienemy is the opposite of the Nurturing Friend.

ATTITUDE: The Frienemy is not there *for* you, but she is there to take advantage of you! She might pretend to like you as long as *other people* in your group like you.

NICKNAME: The Double Agent, the User, Me-Me.

WARNING: The Frienemy is probably friends with one of your *real* friends, so you just have to tolerate her. She will know some of your secrets, which makes her a possible "mean note writer."

CLOTHING: Whatever you have in your closet seems to look good on her . . . She loves to borrow stuff and hates to return it!

TRADEMARK LINE: "If my mom calls for me at your house, tell her I'm there and that I'll call her right back. Then call me on my cell and let me know."

LET'S CELEBRATE! March 9th is National Backstabbers' Day.

The Athlete

A tomboy is a *girl*. Go figure!

ATTITUDE: One of the coolest things about the Athlete is that her self-esteem isn't wrapped up in how she looks or what other people think about her. She has her own interests and friends. She usually has good energy and encourages others. The Athlete is disciplined, but because she is used to doing things her way, she can be stubborn.

CLOTHING: The Athlete will come to school in a soccer or lacrosse outfit, and if someone doesn't like it, it's just tough luck. Non-girly clothes are more practical!

TRADEMARK LINE: "Think fast!"

FUN FACT: The term "tomboy" dates all the way back to 1562. It could mean a rude boy (apparently a kid named Tom was sort of a jerk back then) or "a girl who enjoys rough noisy activities, like a boy." Shakespeare refers to tomboys in one of his plays.

Supergirl

Some girls are genuinely nice, beautiful people. Supergirls have such high self-esteem, they don't worry about what others think of them.

ATTITUDE: Supergirl will sit with pretty much anyone at lunch. She is friendly and smiles easily. She wants everyone to feel as good about themselves as she feels about herself.

NICKNAMES: Prom-Queen, Miss Congeniality.

LIKES: Being a good listener to other people, including everybody in her group.

SURPRISING FACT: Even though everyone loves Supergirl, she may be really hard on herself in private.

Girlie Girl

This is the girl who was born wearing a pink outfit and a princess crown.

ATTITUDE: She is the sweetest! Girly Girls don't walk; they float and bounce. Things that can distract them include flowers, little animals, rainbows, candy, and babies.

ALIASES: Little Fluffy Froufrou, H.R.H. (Her Royal Highness).

CLOTHING: She likes summer dresses; t-shirts with puppy dogs, rainbows, and unicorns on them; blouses and skirts with flowers on them. She may have a tiara hidden in her locker.

LIKES: Speaking in a high-pitched, singsong style.

74

TRADEMARK LINE: "Sugar and spice and everything nice!"

DISLIKES: No profanity EVER.

HEROES: Little Bo-Peep, the Little Mermaid.

FUN FACT: Girlie Girl may be a Creative Genius in hiding. See if you can borrow a unicorn sticker or a fuzzy pen and really get to know her.

Creativity Girl

She's the queen of art, poetry, and fashion!

ATTITUDE: Creative Girl can express herself in so many ways. Maybe she makes her own earrings or clothes, or styles her own hair (which, last you looked, was dyed green), or has a black belt in karate, or does needlework.

CLOTHING: Creative Girl can come to school with a far-out look and pull it off! That's because she has *style*.

75

TRADEMARK LINE: "My hair is chartreuse today. Do you like it?"

BEWARE! If you stand next to Creative Girl and don't move, she will either paint you a different color or cover you in papier mâché. Also, look out if she's holding pipe cleaners, fabric swatches, or glitter.

Goth Girl

Gothic fashion got started in the early 1980s by musicians who wanted to be seen as sad, wistful, and gloomy.

ATTITUDE: Goth Girl will be sarcastic, especially about things she really likes. It's fun for her to pretend to be a romantic, misunderstood loner. ***Optional version***: Theatrical and dramatic!

FASHION: Black clothing, black hair, and white face makeup. Big boots. Some black eyeliner and as many piercings as her parents will allow. Overcoats are good; capes are better.

EXTRA CREDIT: Rebel Goths wear white lipstick and T-shirts that say "Choose Life."

NICKNAMES: Night Angel, Raven, Princess Darkness, you get the idea.

IF YOU WANT TO SCARE HER, SAY: "I took your black lipstick."

LIKES: Candles. Tim Burton movies. Keanu Reeves in The Matrix. Ann Rice.

DISLIKES: Bright colors, pink candy hearts, khakis, and daylight. And no sports, ever!

INTERESTING FACT: Goths get their name from an ancient tribe of German barbarians who actually did not wear much black.

They preferred animal furs and turtle-neck sweaters.

Funny Girl

Anytime you need the mood lightened, she's the one to have around.

ATTITUDE: She can make fun of almost anything!

NICKNAMES: The Class Clown.

TRADEMARK LINE: "Hahahahahaha. Oh, HA!"

LIKES: Funny Girl is never too shy or embarrassed to make silly faces or dance in front of the class. She laughs at herself if she is the butt of a joke, or even if she is in a bit of trouble with the teacher.

DISLIKES: People who don't laugh at her Funny Girl jokes.

INTERESTING FACT: Because Funny Girl is often thinking of the next funny thing she's going to say, she's not always the best listener.

The Drama Queen

Life is so much more exciting with the Drama Queen around. For her, the world is a stage, and she will make every scene in her life thrilling and theatrical.

ATTITUDE: The Drama Queen wants information about everybody! When you see her in the hallway, she will be walking next to a friend and downloading dirt about "who did what to whom."

TRADEMARK LINE: "I shouldn't say anything, but . . ."

NICKNAMES: The Inside Scoop, The Grapevine.

LIKES: Exaggerating and freaking out, no matter what the topic is: "Oh my GOD, I love gum! It's SOOO good!"

79

DISTURBING FACT: Since the Drama Queen will say bad things about *other* people behind their backs, remember that she will probably say bad things about *you* behind your back.

USEFUL FACT: Because the Drama Queen loves drama, she will *create* the drama herself if there seems to be a shortage.

The Leader Who Makes a Difference

She's going to be part of the solution!

ATTITUDE: Go, go, go! The Leader Who Makes a Difference isn't bossy; instead she leads by example.

TRADEMARK LINE: "Let's do it!"

NICKNAMES: President [*insert-her-name-here*].

LIKES: Devoted to making the world a better place, the Leader is going to house the homeless, feed the foodless, and clothe the . . . never mind.

80

DISLIKES: People who are downers.

INTERESTING FACT: The Leader might be more of an *authority figure* for her friends than their own teachers or parents. This isn't a bad thing. Dedicated Leaders are actually sincere, which is one reason they're so special.

The Boy-Crazy Guy Magnet

Some girls prefer to hang out with guys.

ATTITUDE: Boys rule.

FASHION: Whatever jacket her current boyfriend has.

TRADEMARK LINE: "Oh look, there's Mark! Gotta go!"

INTERESTING FACT: The Boy-Crazy Guy Magnet is somebody who doesn't like to be alone.

STRANGE FACT: Although you may be surprised, the Boy-Crazy Guy Magnet

81

may be unhappy that she doesn't have more girlfriends. A girl who is *really* boy-crazy *might* still be finding her own identity.

The Silent Genius

If a brain surgeon and a rocket scientist had kids, this is the result!

ATTITUDE: The Silent Genius likes to observe the world around her; she may take notes in a journal or doodle artwork compulsively. Whether she gets good grades or not, she has her own brilliant insights.

FASHION: The Silent Genius often doesn't care about fashion at all.

NICKNAMES: Study-aholic, Brainiac.

LIKES: The Silent Genius may focus on schoolwork or her own creative projects as opposed to being social.

FUN FACT: By concentrating on her mind and education while young, the Silent Genius is often the most successful girl later in life.

The Cling-On

Static electricity has nothing on her.

ATTITUDE: It's hard for a girl to know where she belongs in middle school and high school. Because of this, some girls end up trying way too hard to stick with a social group.

ALIASES: The Agreeing Machine, the Wanna-Be, the Copy Cat, the Yes Girl.

CLOTHING: What's everyone else wearing?

LEAST FAVORITE HOLIDAY: Independence Day.

TRADEMARK LINE: "What are you guys talking about? Where are you going? Can I come?"

GOOD TO KNOW: Because of her social insecurity, it is easy to be tough on the Cling-On. *Don't be.* She may be cool one-on-one; give her a chance to show her real personality.

★ Studies really do show that the social groups girls are in will eventually play a huge role on their grades. Who you hang out with will influence how hard you work at your education.

The Imaginary Friend

When the pressures of having actual friends are too much, just make up your own!

ATTITUDE: Should be pretty good. After all, if the Imaginary Friend has a bad attitude, it's *your* fault!

NOTE WRITING TIP: If you write your Imaginary Friend any notes, it is usually better to use invisible ink, so nobody who's "real" thinks you're nutty.

FUN FACT: Imaginary Friends don't argue much. If your imaginary friend *does* argue with you, it may be time to end the friendship. If you're not sure how to do this, just use your imagination.

The Friend You Should Make Today

It's easy to look at people and pick apart what's wrong with them. If it seems like everyone has something wrong with them, that's because it's true! There are no perfect people, so judging them by their outside image is judging them unfairly.

Only about half of all girls say they liked their best friends the first time they met them. This means that half of all girls *didn't* like their best friends when they first met! If you get to know any "type" of girl, you start understanding how unique she is. She's not weird, she's funny. Or maybe she's not stuck on herself, she's just shy. You'll never know unless you give her a chance.

SISTERHOOD IS POWERFUL! Try to think good thoughts toward other girls, even if those girls are really different than you. Growing up is tough for everybody. If girls stuck up for each other more and dissed each other less, you *know* the world would be a much better place.

★ "One who looks for a friend without faults will have none." —*Hasidic proverb*

Cliques (pronounced "clicks") and Popularity

Social groups, or "cliques," are never more important to a girl's world than during 5th through 8th grades. Cliques do exist in high school, college, and even the adult

Best Friend Test

So, she's your best friend, huh? We'll see about that right now!

1. When is her birthday?
2. What makes her really mad?
3. What is her favorite food?
4. Where was she born?
5. What is her middle name?
6. If she could be an animal, what kind would she be?
7. What is her blood type? (JK)
8. Who does she want to marry?
9. What does she want to be when she grows up?
10. How many pairs of socks does she own?

★ SCORING ★

After checking with your friend to see how you did, see the scoring guide below!

1-3 correct: Liar! You don't even know her!
4-6 correct: You might be her good friend, but her BEST friend?
7-9 correct: You ARE her best friend!
10 correct: You are either a genius or a stalker! ☺

world, but it's in middle school that girls start to get used to the idea of being in a social group.

Maybe you don't need that many friends. Having *one* best friend keeps things simple, because you don't have to spend a lot of time figuring out what to do together. On the other hand, if you have *two* best friends, the three of you will always have something to talk about ... namely, each other!

But if you have a *lot* of friends, things will always be complicated and they'll never be boring! Girls like the security of being in a group at a time when everything seems topsy-turvy. But hanging out with a group of friends often brings up issues of popularity, both within the group and with other groups. Popularity (whatever that is!) often belongs to the girls who are most admired or most feared (or both!).

You may think that you're *not* in a clique. And maybe you're right! But if you've had the same group of friends for a long time, that's pretty much what a clique is.

But cliques aren't necessarily **bad.** A clique can be a blessing because growing up is tough to do, and it's nice to have the support of good friends who are going through the same things you are. Plus, you can have a few good friends in the clique and then other, more casual friends also. As the friendships shift and little arguments break out between people, you can shift your friendships around a little and still have the safety of the group.

WARNING! Don't ever go to a horror movie with a bunch of your friends! This would be a Sick Chick Flick Clique. Many states have outlawed these groups.☺

But cliques can become a curse if gossip, rumors, backstabbing, and jealousy become a part of the way the group operates. This is pretty weird because girls are in cliques because they *want friends,* so why would they want to hurt anybody?

If you're wondering if your clique is good or evil, think about how you feel away from it. Do your friends make your life better or more of a drama? Do you feel as strong *away* from your friends as you do *with* your friends?

If a clique fight breaks out, it can get ugly. For some reason, a girl in a clique fight will try to create an "army" for herself. Somehow the winner will be the girl who has more girls on **HER** side.

WE'RE ALL FRIENDS!

ELIZABETH IS BEST FRIENDS WITH HANNAH. BUT SHE'S ALSO BEST FRIENDS WITH ISABELLA, MADDY, AND ME. BUT MADDY AND ME ARE REALLY BEST FRIENDS, ALONG WITH MARIA AND ISABELLA. ACTUALLY, MARIA DOESN'T THINK ISABELLA IS HER BEST FRIEND. BUT ISABELLA THINKS MARIA IS HER BEST FRIEND. MARIA THINKS THAT HANNAH IS HER BEST FRIEND, BUT AS YOU KNOW, THAT'S ACTUALLY ELIZABETH. SEE?

Questions That Girls in Cliques Ask Themselves

"WHAT'S MY ROLE IN THIS GROUP?"

"WHO TOOK MY LIP GLOSS?"

"DO I HAVE TOO MANY FRIENDS?"

"WHICH ONE OF US IS PRETTIEST (OR SMARTEST, BEST-DRESSED, NICEST, ETC.)?"

If someone tries to recruit you into her **Clique Army,** avoid her, or if it's remotely possible, try to make peace. (You just *know* the fight is over something stupid like a miscommunication, or an argument about whether pink is cooler than black.)

Some cliques seem to exist only to tell the secrets of other people. Even though this is clearly wrong, it's hard to resist a secret. There is something about things that are supposed to be "secret" that

91

Are You in a Clique?

1. WATCH how people come to your group. Is it easy for a person to join your group at lunch without it being a big deal? Is it possible for a person to leave your group without there being any drama?

2. LOOK at the people in your group of friends. Is it possible that any of the girls like the other members of the group just because of their clothes, looks, or popularity?

3. LISTEN to the conversations that the people around you have. Is most of the talk about appearances? (How to look good, who looks good, who doesn't look good, hey I look good, etc.)

makes them more interesting. Even the most boring story is suddenly glamorous and charming if it is a *secret!*

Secrets!

"SECRETS, SECRETS ARE NO FUN UNLESS YOU SHARE WITH EVERYONE!"
—*Lynn Adair*

Many experts think that the ability to keep a secret is the sign of a healthy mind. Starting about the age of 6 or 7, kids begin to understand the idea of keeping a secret, and in some cases, the idea of being trustworthy. So don't expect a little kid to be able to keep a secret. They just don't get it! A seven-year-old girl named Laura said it all: "I know what a secret is. It's something you only tell *one* person at a time!"

We think there are three kinds of secret keepers:

THE VAULT: This girl can keep a secret, and she *does!* If a secret goes in, it will never come out again. She is a very rare breed. If you have a "vault" for a girlfriend, you're fortunate. When you're going to pop unless you tell someone something, this is the girlfriend to talk to.

THE PIGGY BANK: These girls can keep a secret, but if someone pressures them, they will "break" open and spill their change—we mean secrets—all over the place. Although some of us are stronger Piggy Banks than others, most of us are in this category.

THE OPEN DOOR: This girl will keep a secret for up to an hour sometimes. Then she just can't help herself! But if you're lucky, she might only tell her secret to one person at a time.

Which one are you? If you're honest with yourself, and you don't want to get in trouble, just 'fess up next time someone is getting ready to spill the beans!

TIP: If you really are going to explode unless you tell someone a burning secret, and there are no Vaults available, try a pet. Most animals are trustworthy, although guinea pigs do have a bad reputation. You could also tell a parent or someone who lives in another town.

That way the secret is **out** (whew!), but nobody will *find out* (probably).

One thing we've always wondered about is when one of our friends wants to know one of *our* secrets. Sometimes a friend will even say that she has a "right" to know your secret. This has always cracked us up—unless the secret has to do with a life-or-death situation, or the person is a law-enforcement officer, nobody has a right to know *your* secrets!

★ *"Eavesdropping"* means to *listen in on a conversation you're not a part of.* In England during the 1400s, eavesdropping was a crime that a person could be thrown into jail for!

Gossip

"THE LESS YOU TALK ABOUT OTHERS, THE MORE PEOPLE WILL LISTEN IF YOU DO."
—Ebola Jones

Gossip is what happens when two or more people talk about someone who isn't there. You already know that gossip is *bad,* but it is also unavoidable. Girls just love to talk about other people! Check out these amazing gossip facts:

★ *85 percent of gossip is about friends or acquaintances.* (So you can plan that people are going to gossip about you sometime soon!)

★ **65 percent of gossip reflects badly on the person being talked about.** (So 35 percent of gossip is positive or neutral!)

★ **55 percent of gossipers pass on to others whatever gossip they hear.** (The juicier the gossip, the more likely it will be passed along.)

★ **28 percent of gossipers tell four or more people their gossip.** (This is how gossip can start off true but quickly get exaggerated or changed.)

Studies also show that people who are in a positive mood or who have high self-esteem usually pass along *positive* news about others. People who are feeling low tend to spread negative gossip about others.

Gossip is really addictive. This might be because everyone knows that gossip is almost never accurate. So hearing some gossip is sort of like getting a piece in a puzzle. If you can just get enough pieces, you can solve the mystery of what really happened!

How do you avoid gossip? You can't. It's *impossible!* BUT you can try to avoid contributing to negative gossip. Let's say you're in a big group of girls. The gossip starts, and you're being practically invited to say something bad about another person behind her back. Here are some good neutral things to say:

"I DON'T KNOW HER VERY WELL."

"WHO WANTS GUM?"

"IT'S NONE OF MY BUSINESS."

"HAS ANYONE SEEN MY LOOFAH?"

"SHE HAS HER LIFE, AND I HAVE MINE."

OR,

JUST SHRUG AND ROLL YOUR EYES.

★ *DANGER!* During a thunderstorm, it IS possible for lightning to travel through phone lines, which can electrocute someone talking on the phone! It happens rarely, but if a girl is on a corded phone, it is a possibility.

Fun Stuff!

TO DO

"ANYTHING, EVERYTHING, LITTLE OR BIG BECOMES AN ADVENTURE WHEN THE RIGHT PERSON SHARES IT."
—*Kathleen Norris*

It used to be that girls grew up to be homemakers, mothers, and cooks. Many women still are all those things, but nowadays, girls can also grow up to be astronauts, police officers, doctors, senators, even mailmen. Or should we say mail**women.** (Okay, ***letter carriers!***) A girl can be whatever she wants to be! ☺

Hobbies

Trying new things (or old things in a different way) is what life is all about. If you don't already have a hobby or interest that makes you unique, get one! It could be related to cooking, sports, music, collecting, crafts, writing, painting, photography, community service, or anything you can imagine. Just try something *new.* Having a unique interest will set you apart from the pack and allow you to enjoy your "alone time" so you won't spend it worrying about what everyone else is doing.

Maybe you *are* interested in things that some people might think are stereotypical for girls. Take it to the next level! Be creative. Do you like buying clothes? Try *making* them! Maybe you will want to grow up to *design* them. Do you like to sing? Get a karaoke machine or join a choir. Maybe you will grow up to be a performance artist (okay, we all know you want to be a rock star!), or maybe you will teach voice lessons or become a speech therapist. If you think jewelry is fun to wear, take a class in designing and creating it. You can even start your own business selling it.

A great way to express yourself is to **make your own Web site or blog.** There are lots of free places where you can construct your own site, and you don't have to learn HTML (computer code) to do it. Don't get suckered into actually paying money at these places. Be sure to go for the "free" options as you make your choices. You can use your creativity to design your Web site to reflect you.[1]

If you start by thinking about what you **LOVE** to do, you're probably on the right track to finding your hobby. We're assuming that you know about classic activities like Cat's Cradle (and other

---

1. *Remember not to put your address or phone number on your site so you'll be safe and worry-free.*

string games), face painting, tie-dying
T-shirts, and outer-space exploration. ☺

Activities

While you're figuring out your new passion,
take a look at some of the following activities. We have listed them from the easiest
to the most challenging.

Arm Shortening

Talk about being limber!

YOU WILL NEED: A wall, an arm, a hand at
the end of the arm, fingers.

1. *FACE A WALL. STAND UP STRAIGHT!*

2. *EXTEND AN ARM AND MOVE YOUR FEET UNTIL YOUR
FINGERS JUST TOUCH THE WALL.*

3. *KEEPING YOUR ARM STRAIGHT, BRING IT DOWN AND
BEHIND YOU.*

4. *NOW BRING YOUR ARM BACK UP TO ITS ORIGINAL
POSITION. IT'S SHORTER!*

Want to know why this works? (Come on, you do, don't you?) See the bottom of the page.[2]

The Ultimate Makeover

How much do you trust your friends?

YOU WILL NEED: A friend who is a good sport, makeup supplies for the face (no mascara!), a blindfold.

THIS IS A SUPER-HILARIOUS IDEA. YOU NEED AT LEAST TWO GIRLS TO PLAY, ALTHOUGH AUDIENCE MEMBERS WILL GET A HUGE KICK OUT OF IT.

The two girls sit and face each other. One girl will apply makeup to the other's face, but the trick is that the girl applying the makeup has to do it blindfolded! That's why it's important that the makeup be safe to use on the face, especially if it accidentally gets on the lips or eyes.

---

2. *You unconsciously lean toward the wall while bringing your arm back and then forward again.*

Quick Summer Fun!

If you have access to a swimming pool, drag a kid's inflatable pool over to it. (Just blow it up, but don't put any water in it.) You can use the inflatable pool like a boat inside the larger pool!

The audience can gather around and watch (no hints!) as the blindfolded girl applies makeup. When she's done, the two girls switch roles, but nobody is allowed to look in the mirror until both are done. *Then* they can look!

OPTION: A different version of this game is getting a supply of hairclips, barrettes, combs, and brushes and having the girls do each other's hair.

105

Multi-Tasking

A new twist on doing two things at once!

YOU WILL NEED: A foot and a hand.

It is commonly believed that girls are better at multi-tasking than boys. Let's test that! Sit down. Lift your right foot off the floor. Start making clockwise circles in the air with your foot.

Good! Now keep circling your foot and hold your left hand in the air in front of you. Pretend that you are going to use your finger to make a number "6" in the air in front of you.

Now put the two parts together! Circle your right foot clockwise and make a "6" in the air with your left hand. Tough, huh? If you're like most girls, your foot will change directions even though you don't want it to. Try experimenting with different hand-and-foot combinations and directions.

Money Magic

This trick will make you richer! (In a very general, non-money way.)

YOU WILL NEED: A dollar bill, two paper clips.

Take a dollar bill (or any other denomination) and fold it as the illustration shows. Then put the paperclips on the bill as shown. Tell your audience to get ready, and then quickly pull the ends of the dollar bill apart from each other. The

paper clips will fly up and when they come down, they will be magically connected!

Contagious Yawns on Demand

Just open wide . . . soon everyone else will too!

YOU WILL NEED: A mouth and a group of people.

You know that people yawn when they are bored or tired. There are other reasons to yawn; lots of us yawn when we're nervous! But strangely, people also yawn just because they saw someone else yawn first. (You may even yawn just *reading* about yawns!) These are called *contagious yawns.*

One out of two people who see someone else yawn will usually open wide and yawn themselves. To test this theory, try yawning in a subtle (but noticeable) way when you are with a group of people. See if anyone else then yawns in the next thirty seconds.

Now, here's the cool part. People who imitate someone else's yawns (without thinking about it) are more ***empathetic*** than most. That means that they are ***sensitive*** to other people and their feelings. Watch who yawns and make a mental note: They are ***sensitive!***

Make a Dork Album

Celebrate your inner dork!

YOU WILL NEED: Embarrassing pictures of yourself and/or a friend, a small picture album.

Round up the worst, least flattering photos of yourself you can find. You know, the pictures where your eyes are closed, where you didn't know someone was going to take a picture, where you just woke up in the morning, or where you made a horrible face on purpose but then were surprised at just how horrible it was . . . ***those pictures!*** Then sort through them and pick the cream of the dorkiest photos.

Once you have your All-Star Lineup, fill a small photo album with them. This will provide you with laughs when you may be taking life too seriously. These also make *great* gifts for friends! You can make them a Dork Album of just your friend, just you, or both of you together.

Dress-Up Day!

Tired of playing a joke on one person at a time?

YOU WILL NEED: Friends.

Persuade all your friends that they simply ***must*** dress up in a certain style on a particular day. It could be Hawaiian or 1960s or mismatched clothing—but have a theme and really push for it.

Then when the "Dress-Up Day" rolls around, just wear your regular clothing. When you see your friends at school in their floral shirts or tie-dye, they will be surprised. "Why aren't you dressed up? This was YOUR idea!" they will ask. Act

very casual and say, "I changed my mind."
Their expressions will give you laughs
for a long time. (Hopefully, they won't be
mad at you for a long time, too!)

Chain, Chain, Chain ... Chain of Daisies

Organic jewelry has never been better!

YOU WILL NEED: Daisies, a pocket knife.
(Other long-stemmed flowers can also
work, even dandelions.)

111

You can make a ***daisy-crown*** with this method, which may be the coolest thing of all time. Other possibilities include daisy belts, daisy bracelets, daisy anklets, and daisy chokers. ("Hey, get these daisies off of me!") You may need as many as 35 to 40 daisies for a belt, but fewer for other daisy chains.

Cut a daisy stem so that it's about 3 to 4 inches long. Cut a small slit about halfway down the stem; then do the same thing with the remaining flowers.

Take a daisy and stick its stem through the hole of one of the other daisies. Then take another daisy and put it into the hole of the daisy you just stuck through the first one. Keep doing that! Work your way along, testing for length and straightening the stems, until you only have one daisy left. Then hook that into your first daisy. Put on your crown and find something to use for a throne. The woodland creatures will soon be there to pay respect and compliment you on your beauty.

NOTE: DON'T USE ROSES FOR THIS. THINK OF THE THORNS!

★ The word daisy originally meant "day's eye." So that means the petals are the flower's eyelashes! Cute!

Fortune-Teller Note

What? You've never made one of these?

YOU WILL NEED: A square piece of paper, a pen or pencil.

In case you've never folded up a fortune-teller, here's how to do it:

1. *FIRST UP, GET A SQUARE PIECE OF PAPER. THEN JUST FOLD IT IN HALF. NOW UNFOLD IT.*

2. *FOLD EACH OF THE FOUR CORNERS OF THE PAPER TO THE CENTER POINT. LEAVE THEM FOLDED DOWN, AND TURN THE PAPER OVER.*

3. *ON THE BACK SIDE OF THE FOLDED PIECE OF PAPER, TAKE EACH OF THE FOUR CORNERS AND FOLD THEM DOWN TO THE CENTER POINT. THEN NUMBER EACH OF THE EIGHT TRIANGULAR FOLDS.*

113

4. *NOW YOU NEED EIGHT FORTUNES. YOU NEED TO INVENT THESE. IN ADDITION TO "YES" AND "NO" TYPE ANSWERS, YOU MAY WANT TO HAVE SOME "MAYBE" AND "RANDOM" FORTUNES. FOR EXAMPLE, YOU COULD HAVE FORTUNES THAT READ:*

We sense an answer in the air . . .
what does the wind whisper?
The future holds great promise.
Who're you kidding, sister?
Popsicles are good!
Go ask the Magic-8 Ball®!
Possible but not probable.
You know the answer in your heart.
Absolutely yes.
Not a chance!

WRITE THESE FORTUNES UNDER THE TRIANGLES WITH THE NUMBERS.

5. *THEN TURN THE PAPER OVER AND WRITE THE NAME OF A COLOR OVER EACH OF THE SQUARES. PRESTO-CHANGE-O! YOU'RE READY TO START FORTUNE-TELLING!*

Show a friend the colors she has to pick from. After she picks one of the four colors,

Fold in half

unfold

Fold 4 corners into center

flip over and fold 4 corners into center

number each triangle

Label with fortunes

flip over and Label with colors

turn the "color" side of the fortune teller down. Stick a thumb and forefinger into "pinching position" on each side.

You will start spelling out the color, opening and closing the fortune-teller with each letter. Once you finish, have your friend pick one of the four numbers that are revealed on the *inside* of the fortune-teller.

115

Again, open and close the fortune-teller as many times as the number she picked. Your friend again picks one of the four visible interior numbers, and this is the fortune that you peel back and open. If you follow all these steps, we can say with certainty that the future holds great promise. ☺

It's Different for Girls!

This experiment often demonstrates the natural superiority of girls!

YOU WILL NEED: one male human (ten years old or older), one female human (ten years old or older), one or two lip-gloss, ChapStick, or lipstick containers.

1. HAVE YOUR GIRL AND BOY VOLUNTEERS KNEEL DOWN ON THE FLOOR. MAKE SURE THAT THEY KEEP THEIR LEGS TOGETHER.

2. NOW, HAVE BOTH OF THEM BEND FORWARD AND PUT THEIR ELBOWS UP AGAINST THEIR KNEES. THEIR FOREARMS SHOULD EXTEND FORWARD FROM THE KNEES, AND THEIR PALMS SHOULD BE FLAT

*AGAINST THE FLOOR. (THEIR LEGS SHOULD STILL BE
TOGETHER.)*

3. *PLACE THE LIP-GLOSS CONTAINERS (OR WHATEVER
   YOU'RE USING) UPRIGHT AT THE END THEIR
   FINGERS.*

4. *OKAY, NOW YOU'RE READY! HAVE BOTH OF THEM NOW
   KNEEL UP STRAIGHT WITH LEGS STILL TOGETHER.
   HAVE THEM CLASP THEIR HANDS BEHIND THEIR
   BACKS, ABOVE THEIR WAISTS.*

5. *NOW TELL THEM THIS: "KEEPING YOUR ARMS AND
   LEGS IN POSITION, LEAN FORWARD, KNOCK THE
   LIP-GLOSS CONTAINER OVER WITH YOUR NOSE, AND
   RETURN TO THE KNEELING UP POSITION."*

WATCH! The odds are very high that the
girl can do it. The odds are very high that
the boy can't!

The reason this happens is because girls
tend to have their body weight down lower
than boys. They can balance better!

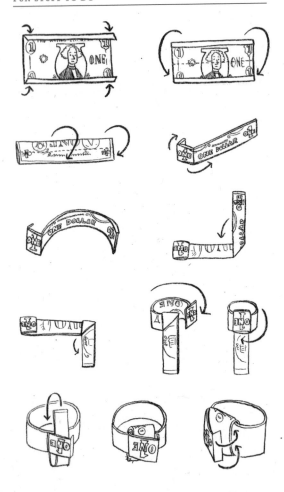

Dollar Ring

How to make a bling-bling ring!

YOU WILL NEED: Any U.S. paper money.

If you're looking for a fun way to "wear" your lunch money, this is it. Girls have been using this design for a long time; it dates back to at least the 1930s!

1. *TAKE A DOLLAR BILL (THE CRISPER, THE BETTER) AND FOLD THE WHITE BORDER ON THE TOP AND BOTTOM OVER TO THE FRONT SIDE.*

2. *THEN FOLD THE BILL EXACTLY IN HALF, LENGTHWISE. OKAY? NOW DO IT AGAIN! (SO YOU FOLD THE BILL IN HALF TWICE LENGTHWISE.) THE BIG ONE INSIGNIA SHOULD BE FRAMED BY YOUR FOLD.*

3. *HOLD THE BILL IN FRONT OF YOU. ON THE LEFT END, FOLD THE WHITE BORDER OF THE END BACK AND AWAY FROM YOU. GOOD! NOW MAKE ANOTHER FOLD THE SAME WAY THAT FRAMES THE PICTURE OF THE ONE.*

4. START TURNING THE FOLDED BILL INTO THE SHAPE AS SHOWN; YOU MAY WANT TO WRAP IT AROUND YOUR FINGER TO GIVE IT THE SHAPE YOU'LL WANT. MAKE SURE IT LOOKS LIKE THE PICTURE!

5. WITH THE FOLDED END ON THE LEFT, MAKE A FOLD SO THAT THE RIGHT SIDE OF THE BILL BENDS STRAIGHT UP. THEN WRAP AND FOLD IT OVER AND DOWN AS THE PICTURE SHOWS.

6. YOU'RE ALMOST DONE! LOOP THE FOLDED END (ON YOUR LEFT) AROUND IN A CIRCLE SO THAT THE SYMBOL OF THE ONE ENDS UP RIGHT IN FRONT OF THE FOLDED AREA THAT YOU MADE WITH STEP 5. THERE SHOULD BE A LITTLE TAIL HANGING DOWN BELOW IT.

7. TAKE THE TAIL AND WRAP IT UP AND BEHIND THE FOLDED SYMBOL OF THE ONE. THEN KEEP GOING AROUND AND FOLD IT OVER THE TOP. (IF IT'S REALLY LONG, YOU MAY NEED TO WRAP IT A LITTLE AROUND THE BOTTOM TOO.)

8. TUCK THAT LAST LITTLE FOLD TO THE RIGHT OF THE SYMBOL ONE INTO THE GAP BETWEEN THE FOLDED "BADGE" AND THE RING ITSELF. THIS HOLDS THE WHOLE THING TOGETHER!

FUN STUFF TO DO

9. WALK AROUND LIKE YOU'RE COOL!

★ *TIP:* Don't wear your ring around any area with mean people who might want your pretty jewelry!

Black Light Freak-Out

It doesn't seem like this would work that well. It does!

YOU WILL NEED: a black light, Liquid Tide, a bubble blower.

The human eye can't see "black light." You can buy ***black light*** light bulbs; they are sometimes used for taking night photographs or for cool tricks like this. Tide detergent has a fluorescent chemical in it that shows up under black light really well. So here's what you do:

Mix ⅓ cup of Liquid Tide with the same amount of water. Turn on your black light. Dip your bubble blower into your mixture and blow bubbles. They will glow and look purple-freaky! This is a great thing to do at slumber parties and on Halloween.

Soda Blast!

It's dramatic and it's safe.

YOU WILL NEED: A bottle of diet soda (20 ounces minimum), some Mentos breath mints, a pipe or test tube or cardboard roll you can stack the Mentos in.

For best results, let your soda sit at room temperature for a day before you use it, and do not jostle the bottle around. You will want to do this activity outside. The bigger the soda bottle you're using, the more room you will need.

To begin, unroll your Mentos package. Your goal will be to dump all of them into the soda bottle at the same time. The best way to do this is to stack them inside a test tube or short piece of pipe. Hold a small card under them so they don't fall out.

Now slowly open the bottle of soda. Position your stack of Mentos directly over the mouth of the bottle. Remember, you want them all to go in together. When it's all lined up, slide the card away from the bottom of the stack and let them fall in. Then stand back. The contents of the bottle will erupt straight up in an amazing way!

How does it work? All the carbon dioxide in the bottle is attracted to the Mentos. The little bubbles combine to make big bubbles, and the big bubbles combine to make an eruption. There will probably still be soda in the bottle after your blast goes off, so if you have more Mentos, you can do the trick again with the same container of soda.

Journalism

Does calling it a "diary" make it less cool?

YOU WILL NEED: Uh . . . a journal? Your favorite pen.

" . . . IN THE END, I ALWAYS COME BACK TO MY DIARY. IT'S WHERE I START AND FINISH." —*Anne Frank*

As they get older, many girls start looking inward and thinking hard about their lives. They ask the important questions: *Who am I? Who are you? Where did I leave my favorite pen?* This is a time of life when you need a place to record your wishes, secrets, and feelings for yourself.

A journal can be an amazing document to look back over and see what was important to you last year or five years ago. You're basically making your own time capsule! Whether you think you're a good writer or not *doesn't matter*. The journal is for **YOU,** although we bet you'll eventually want to share parts of it with others.

WHERE you actually write may matter. Although it's easy to write on a computer, there is something really personal about a journal that is handwritten. Here are some different ways you can approach your journal:

ABSOLUTELY CREATIVE JOURNAL: Poems, doodles, ideas, sketches, made-up languages, and glued-in collages collide in a beautifully messy work of art and you.

"GET THE BAD JUJU OUT" JOURNAL: This is perfect therapy. If you pour all of your insecurities, fears, and hatred out into your journal, guess what's left inside you? Nothing but good stuff!

GRATITUDE JOURNAL: Think about what you have to be grateful for, and write about how, even during the tough times, life is good.

"BE THANKFUL FOR WHAT YOU HAVE; YOU'LL END UP HAVING MORE. IF YOU CONCENTRATE ON WHAT YOU DON'T HAVE, YOU WILL NEVER, EVER HAVE ENOUGH." —Oprah Winfrey

DECOMPRESSION JOURNAL: By writing down the day's events, you can process through them and gain perspective. Keeping a journal like this is like having a front-row seat at the movie of your life.

JOURNALISTIC JOURNAL: Once you've been writing for a while, you may want to encourage your friends to give you writing or artwork they've done and put it into a "joint journal" or "zine." Zines are do-it-yourself (D.I.Y.) publications, but they don't have to be on paper. Your Web site could be where your zine material is, which is when you stop being a *ziner* and become a *blogger* (web-logger).

Or, you can just combine all of the above ideas into one journal! Try to make time for writing, but don't feel like you need to make an entry every day . . . that turns the journal into a chore, instead of the terrific outlet of fun, detoxing, and creativity for you that it can be.

AND REMEMBER: Just like school yearbooks, the *longer* you have your journal, the more priceless it is!

★ *OOPS, ONE MORE THING!* If you leave your journal out, someone is going to read it. (That's what little brothers are for, right?) So if you're writing private thoughts, it would be best if nobody knew it existed. Be sure to hide the journal in a good spot. Not under the bed or in a drawer. Try the pocket of a jacket that you have in the back of your closet. If it's on the computer, protect it with a password. Or just keep it in another dimension!

Magic Bubbles

This is the coolest bubble activity of all time.

YOU WILL NEED: a bottle of bubbles with bubble blower, a decent-sized cardboard box, a plastic garbage bag, dry ice, work gloves.

WARNING: Don't ever touch dry ice with your skin! Dry ice is so cold (minus 100 degrees F), it will stick to you and freeze. It can severely damage and scar your skin.

All you have to do for this simple and amazing activity is line the inside of your cardboard box with the plastic garbage bag. Then put on your gloves and put the dry ice in the box.

Now start blowing some bubbles and blow them *into* the box. The bubbles will act very unusually; they won't rise *or* fall, they will just hover in the box, changing colors and combining with each other. (This is because dry ice is made of frozen carbon dioxide and the bubbles are lighter than the carbon dioxide gas that is being released.)

★ *BONUS:* When you are done with the dry ice, try breaking off a piece (with your gloves on) and putting it in a glass of water for that cool "scary potion" effect! You can also use dry ice to put into balloons . . . after you put it inside the balloon, tie off the end of the balloon. The balloon will be "blown up" by the dry ice! Cool!

Big glass beads with flat backs look cool on everything. Get some Super Glue and glue some of these to things in your room. We bet you'll love it!

The Magic Jar

YOU WILL NEED: A small glass jar with a metal lid, "light" corn syrup, glitter, beads, plastic figures and doo-dads, glue *(better if it's waterproof),* creativity. **Optional:** Food coloring.

Who doesn't love snow globes? You shake them and watch the little snowflakes come swirling down . . . so pretty! And now, you can make your own version of the magic globe.

The scene that you want to create *inside* of the jar needs to be glued down on the *inside* of the metal lid of the jar. Your scene might be made up of little plastic snowmen, doll heads, lost pieces from board games, or costume jewelry. Provided the items are plastic, they should be fine. So, glue them down to the inside of the lid in whatever arrangement you like.

While the lid dries, put the stuff that you want to "float" in the air into the empty jar. Whatever glitter or beads strike your fancy!

Next, pour an equal amount of light corn syrup and water into the jar. Fill the jar fairly full, but not quite all the way. (If you want to put in a little food coloring to make it look like sky or water, now's the time.)

When you're ready for the moment of truth, put glue around the rim of the jar on the inside of the jar's lid. Screw it on tight, and then leave it alone. It has to dry, so let it! Once it *is* dry, prepare for instant holiday dazzle. Pick up the jar, shake it . . . and let the magic begin!

Mehndi (men-dee) Painting

Give yourself a nonpermanent tattoo!

YOU WILL NEED: a friend, henna powder, tea, lemon or lime juice, sugar or honey, a nonmetal bowl. You also need either a pastry bag or a large plastic ziplock bag.

Ancient Indian body painting is amazing. You can do it yourself, or there are probably artists in your area who can help you get started if you prefer. Henna is used as a skin and hair dye. You can find henna in organic food stores, beauty stores, Indian shops, and many other places. The henna you buy should look like a *green* or *brown* powder. Not black! And the fresher it is, the better it works.

Follow the directions that came with your henna, but also be willing to experiment. You will want to mix your henna and let it sit for a few hours, or even overnight.

Although "recipes" vary, mix the henna powder with some tea and lemon or lime

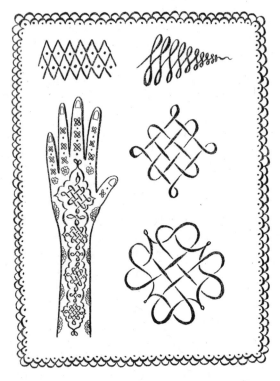

juice in a bowl to make a watery paste. Henna experts are reluctant to give exact amounts, but try starting with a ratio of 2:3 (powder-to-liquid). One way to do it is to make a cup of strong tea and add a little sugar. Then pour some of the tea and lemon juice into the henna powder.

Don't make your henna mix too thick, because the henna mix will "set up" a little bit after you're done. It should be like watery mashed potatoes, with *no* lumps or air pockets.

Once you're done mixing your henna, loosely cover the mixture with cellophane. Some people let the henna sit overnight, but once the surface is darker than the part underneath, the dyes are being released.

When you're ready to paint, either fill up a pastry bag (those things chefs use for frosting) or make your own. Just cut off a tiny bit of the corner of a ziplock freezer bag and carefully pour the paste into the bag. Holding the mix in the bag, squeeze it so that one end makes a small tube. Then start squeezing it out that small corner hole!

If your henna mix is the right consistency, you can also paint it on with a small brush. You can make whatever design you want; there are many good books and Web sites that can give you ideas.

Squeeze or paint the design you want out onto your friend's hand or foot. (If you want to practice with an area nobody will see, try shoulders, backs, or legs.) Many artists dab the henna with a cotton ball dipped in a mix of lemon juice and sugar to help it set up more quickly.

Although mehndi *should* dry for four to six hours, you can do faster versions. (But try to leave the design on as long as possible.) If you don't wash it with water for another four hours, it *can* last for as long as two to three weeks.

★ You can also body paint with glow-in-the-dark paint (craft stores have nontoxic ones) that look really cool in the dark and under black lights. If you want a less permanent body or face paint, mix a little lotion with dry tempera paint.

Crayons!

You might be surprised to learn that these rods of colored wax are more interesting than you think. For example, you know that waxy smell that you get when you open a box of crayons? That smell is *beef fat*. Processed beef fat (called *stearic acid*) is an ingredient in many crayons. The smell of crayons is so well known, a university study found it to be the eighteenth most recognized odor in the nation! (The smell of peanut butter was number two.)

The most famous crayons are probably Crayola crayons. "Crayola" is a word that means "oily chalk." Crayola crayons started out with 8 colors in 1903. Today there are 120 colors. Some of the colors available that you may not have heard about include Outer Space, Manatee, Fuzzy Wuzzy Brown, Dandelion, Eggplant, and Macaroni and Cheese—and you can get them in Glow in the Dark if you want!

Survey Says! A poll of 25,000 Americans found the favorite crayon color of the American people: Blue!

> *"I ALONE CANNOT CHANGE THE WORLD, BUT I CAN CAST A STONE ACROSS THE WATERS TO CREATE MANY RIPPLES."*
> —*Mother Teresa*

Make the World a Better Place

It's time to cast a stone!

YOU WILL NEED: To save the world. (Or at least your hometown.)

This is the most important activity **anybody** can do. When you showed up on this planet, there were problems all over the place. Nobody is blaming you for them, but before you leave, it would be nice if you could help make the world a better place than it was when you found it.

You may already be a member of a club, organization, temple, or church. Maybe you're in Girl Scouts or a Big Sister program. If so, start looking for opportunities to help out. Decide what kinds of issues are important to you. There are also little random things you can do to make

the world better, like smiling or giving someone a compliment. Maybe you've seen the bumper sticker: *COMMIT RANDOM ACTS OF KINDNESS.* That's a great idea!

Besides the good feeling you can get from helping others, making the world a better place also looks great on college applications! Keep track of what you did and when—we guarantee *someone* will be very impressed.

If this sounds like too much for you right now, that's okay. But get around to it sooner or later. We **know** you don't have anything better to do . . . *NOBODY DOES!*

137

Nicknames,

HANDWRITING,
WORDS, AND DOODLES

"A WIFE SHOULD NO MORE TAKE HER HUSBAND'S NAME THAN HE SHOULD HERS. MY NAME IS MY IDENTITY AND MUST NOT BE LOST." —Lucy Stone

Even if you gamble away everything you own playing Candyland, you will always have your name! That is, unless you gamble your name away too . . . but then you would be a *nameless soul*, wandering about without purpose. But *with* your name you have a purpose: to be yourself!

Names are very important to us. Even the quietest kid will correct the teacher if her name is mispronounced during roll on the first day of school. Odds are that *your* name has a rich history and a cool meaning. For example, *Olivia* is a pretty popular name. Who would have guessed that Olivia is the Latin word for "olive"? Amazing! Or how about *Samantha?* This is an ancient name from the Middle East that means "good listener." Cool!

★ When someone tests a new pen, the odds are almost 100 percent that she will write her name with it.

Try looking up your name to learn about it. Also, since your parents picked your name, you should find out why they picked the name they did. Ask them! They may pretend they don't know the information you want, or they might even pretend not to know you. Be persistent!

YOU: WHY DID YOU PICK MY FIRST NAME?

YOUR DAD: I DON'T REMEMBER.

YOU: I SEE. CAN YOU GIVE ME AN EXAMPLE OF SOMETHING ELSE YOU CAN'T REMEMBER?

YOUR DAD: UH . . . WHAT?

YOU: DID YOU LIKE THE SOUND OF MY NAME?

YOUR DAD: YES. YOUR NAME RHYMES WITH PLATYPUS, AND THAT HAS ALWAYS BEEN ONE OF OUR FAVORITE ANIMALS.

OTHER GOOD QUESTIONS TO ASK:

What were the discussions about your name like? Were there *arguments?*

What were some other *possibilities* for your name? (These are always interesting!)

What would your name have been if you were a *boy* instead of a *girl?*

★ A Native American tribe called the Kree names their babies after the first animal the parents see once the child is born.

The Top Ten Most Popular Girl Names

Just like clothes, names go in and out of fashion. What is popular one year isn't popular the next. But there is one girl's name that has been popular for nine years in a row! *Emily* was the number one girl's name from 1996 to 2004.

How many girls do you know with the following names? Here is the most recent list of the top girl's names in the U.S., from number one to number ten:

Emily	*Sophia*
Isabella	*Olivia*
Emma	*Abigail*
Ava	*Hannah*
Madison	*Elizabeth*

Here are the top ten girl's names from back in 1990:

Jessica	*Sarah*
Ashley	*Stephanie*
Brittany	*Jennifer*
Amanda	*Elizabeth*
Samantha	*Lauren*

You want boys, too? Okay, here is the most recent list of the top ten boy's names:

Jacob	*Christopher*
Michael	*Anthony*
Ethan	*William*
Joshua	*Matthew*
Daniel	*Andrew*

There are thousands of girls in the United States named Lexus. What about Porsche?

The Worst Girl Names

After doing a wide survey, we have concluded that these are the worst girl's names:

Bimberly *Pepsi*
Brunhilda *Prunella*
Chinchilla *Rotunda*
Crayola *Salmonella*
Fern *Tamale*
Hortense *Velveeta*
Latrina *Yeti*
Michelina *Zona*
Mossie

No Bad Names Allowed

"WHAT'S IN A NAME? THAT WHICH WE CALL A ROSE

BY ANY OTHER NAME WOULD SMELL AS SWEET."
—*William Shakespeare,* Romeo and Juliet

There was once a fuzzy little fruit from New Zealand that nobody ever ate. It was called the *Chinese gooseberry*. It was so unpopular that someone decided to change the fruit's name to *kiwifruit*. How cute! Sales of the kiwifruit went through the roof, even though the fruit still tasted the same. It was the *name* that made the difference. (The same thing happened to *Hen's Turd Apples*. As soon as they were called *Orange Pippin Apples*, sales improved. Go figure!)

Denmark has the strictest "name laws" of any country in the world. The Danes restrict parents from giving kids any name considered "unusual." This is to prevent kids from getting teased about their names. There are 4,000 approved girl names that parents can choose from. (The boys list only has 3,000!) Babies sometimes remain nameless for months while the parents try to persuade the government to allow a name not on the approved list. Banned names include Pluto, Monkey, and Anus. (Well, that makes sense!) Legal names include Jiminico, Fee, and Molli. The name Tessa is not allowed in Denmark, because *tessa* means "to pee" in Danish.

Celebrity Fake Names

"I ARRIVED IN HOLLYWOOD WITHOUT HAVING MY NOSE FIXED, MY TEETH CAPPED, OR MY NAME CHANGED. THAT IS VERY GRATIFYING TO ME."
—*Barbra Streisand*

People will do almost anything to become famous. Often, one of the first things they do is change their name. Name your favorite actress or music star and the odds are that he or she was born as somebody else, especially if their name sounds too cool to be real. (For example, Vin Diesel was originally Bob Snider.) Maybe their name just changed a little bit, like with Reese Witherspoon. She was born Laura Jean Reese Witherspoon, so she just subtracted a little!

But lots of male music stars go through *big* name changes. Snoop Doggy Dogg was born Calvin Cordozar Broadus, Busta Rhymes was Trevor Smith, and Elton John was Reginald Kenneth Dwight. How about O'Shea Jackson, better known as Ice Cube? But our favorite name change is from an artist known as Ginuwine. His

original name was Elgin Lumpkin. That's
right: *Elgin Lumpkin!*

You can make up fake celebrity names by
imagining what would happen if celebrities got married and combined their
names. If the actress Bea Arthur married
the musician named Sting, she'd be Bea
Sting! What if Snoop Doggy Dogg married
Winnie the Pooh? He'd be Snoop Doggy
Dogg Pooh. ☺

Your Celebrity Name

Since celebrities change their names
around to make them sound better, here's
one way to figure out a new movie star
name for *you*. Take the name of the first
dog you've ever owned. If you've never
owned a dog, take the name of the first
pet your family has ever owned. (Or one
that your parents owned, or the name of
a favorite neighbor's pet. Be creative!)

Now get the name of the first street you ever lived on. If that street is just a number, like 157th Avenue, go with any street NAME that you have lived on or that is near you.

You now have your movie star name! For example, let's say your first pet was a cat named Sheba, and the first street you lived on was York Street. Your movie star name is Sheba York!

This is a lot of fun to do with your friends. You may get a name that sounds like a rich kid (Willow Huntington), an organic Native American (Lima Cherokee), or a strange fairy tale character (Thumbelina Crispin).

Your Letters

The greatest invention of all time is *language*. Once written language was invented, girls could write down their thoughts and feelings. Thousands of years later, people can read what these girls thought and know more about them. This makes written language like a time machine!

And all you need for this time machine are the letters of the alphabet. Our alphabet is usually called the *Roman alphabet,* and it's been around for thousands of years. It is the most commonly used writing system in the world. We are [CLAP-CLAP] Number One!

The Romans thought that each *letter* of their alphabet had important values, so the letters in a child's name were carefully selected because some of the letters were good and some were bad. The letters that were picked to be the *initials* for a name were doubly important because they could affect a kid's future personality.

★ *Alphabet Discrimination!*

There are many different alphabets in the world, but Campbell's Alphabet Soup only comes in the Roman alphabet. This is outrageous! We have a dream that someday, Alphabet Soup will be available in Hebrew, Greek, Arabic, and Hindi alphabets. Maybe we'll leave the Cambodian alphabet out, though. It has 74 letters, and we're not that hungry!

For fun, write out your *full* name (first, middle, and last) and see how you score in the old Roman system of letter values. Put a face score over the letters of your name as you read the score of the letter, and double-score your initials. If you end up with a good score, you rule! (But if you get a bad score, take it easy ... We're pretty sure it doesn't mean anything!)

A is a first-class letter! The Greeks called it alpha, and it is associated with excellence and beginnings. The use of "A" as the top grade on report cards has been around for over a hundred years in the United States. (The letter "a" can also make a lot of different sounds, like in this sentence: *Was Alicia's pa all pale?*) ☺

B is a good letter, but it's always going to be second-best. People with a lot of "Bs" in their name are good at compromising and being team players. Try pinching your nose closed and saying "My mom married my dad." (It'll sound like "By bom buried by dad.") ☺

C is *consistent,* but not that great. Heck, it's only average! One thing it has going for it is that it can make more sounds than any other letter in the alphabet. Say *Circus cheese from the ocean* out loud and you'll see what we mean. ☺

D The Romans thought D was the letter of lazy people! It shows low energy and lack of motivation. Sorry! ☹

E is the most commonly used letter in writing. It also stands for optimism and looking at the positive side of things. ☺

F is the only letter used in report card grades that stands for something. "Failure!" Rats. Back in Roman days, people thought that "F" stood for violence too. ☹

G is a letter of energy and activity. Some might say "hyperactivity"! For people who like to move and travel, this is a ☺.

H If you want to succeed in life, H is the letter for you. It shows ambition and the desire to get ahead. ☺

I There is a reason why the word "I" stands for one's own self. It's because I is the most selfish of the letters! Although people who are self-centered may like it, the rest of us say ☹!

J The letter J is an indicator of a good memory and a healthy outlook on life. It also shows a person who is fair-minded. ☺

K *Money, money, money!* The letter K has symbolized cash for a long time. (In slang, "K" refers to a thousand dollars.) Although money can be good, it also reflects greed and being too caught up in possessions. ☹

L For girls who like sports or challenging mind games, this is a great letter. L is the letter of being coordinated, both physically and mentally. Keeping your balance is important! ☺

M This is a tough letter. On the one hand, the M shows a person who appreciates beauty, but on the other hand, that person may be too hung up on appearances. The "M" is a little too shallow, judging a book by its cover. ☹

N shows a lack of confidence or self-esteem. This letter needs to buck up and believe in itself! ☹

O what a great letter this is! It is also a very feminine letter. It shows deep emotion and feeling, and a strong sensitivity to other people. Girls with a lot of "Os" in their names make great friends, sisters, and mothers. ☺

P The P person is the one who goes along with the crowd. It's the letter that doesn't like to speak up or take risks. ☹

Q is a good letter for learners and teachers, and anyone else who wants to get educated and then pass along her knowledge. (It is also a moody letter, but let's not get hung up on details!) ☺

R U ready for one of the greatest of all letters? "R" is a letter that reflects wisdom, good judgment, and a desire to learn. ☺

S can do a lot of things: Listen to its different sounds: *his, hiss, sure.* Sheesh! Anyway, the top half of "S" is the opposite of the bottom part, so it contains its own opposite, sort of like an alphabetical yin/yang symbol. "S" was thought of as the letter of complexity and goodness. ☺

T Even though T is the second-most used letter in writing, being popular doesn't make it good. "T" is a letter that can't be counted on. It's inconsistent and flaky. ☹

U are number 1! Well, maybe not number 1, but "U" is certainly up there. It is a great letter for a girl, as it is a letter of protection and caring. When picking a babysitter, parents should always go with the girl who has a lot of "Us" in her name! ☺

V We don't know if you are a spiritual person, but if you have a V for an initial, you might be. The "V" shows great instincts and an ability to see what others don't. Don't worry, though, it's not *psycho,* it's *psychic.* ☺

W is dependable, but maybe a bit boring. ☺

X Ever wonder why X is the letter of the *unknown* in math class? It's because this is the most mysterious letter of all. It is also associated with women, because back when you were inside your mother, something called an "XX sex chromosome" decided that you'd be a girl! ☺

Y Some girls don't need to be the center of attention. Why? We don't know! But the letter Y is for girls who don't mind being quiet, thoughtful, and a good friend to others. ☺

Z Maybe because the letter Z doesn't get used a lot, it shows an appreciation for the weird, strange, and out-of-the-ordinary. ☺

★ A to Zed! Even though we pronounce "z" as "zee" in the United States, it is pronounced "zed" in Britain and most Commonwealth countries.

So, how did your name score?

Nicknames

Everyone has to be given a nickname at one point in her life. It's practically a law! Maybe you're a kid who got stuck with a really bad nickname like "Poo-Poo Head" or "Pony Girl." How embarrassing! But still, it's usually better to have a nickname than not. Somehow, nicknames make us seem more colorful and fun.

★ About a thousand years ago, the king of Denmark was nicknamed Eric the Memorable. Today, nobody remembers why.

Here are a few ways that you can come up with nicknames everyone will remember.

To make up a nickname, pick a *first* name from the official state symbols listed on pages 158–160. For your *last* name, pick from the list of cool place names on pages 160–162! (All place names are actual countries or cities.)

STATE SYMBOLS

Apple *(flower, Arkansas)*

Azalea *(wildflower, Georgia)*

Blossom *(flower, Florida)*

Bluestem *(grass, Illinois)*

Boomer *(reptile, Oklahoma)*

Brook *(fish, New York)*

Calico *(cat, Maryland)*

Camellia *(flower, Alabama)*

Chanterelle *(fungus, Oregon)*

Coral *(gem, West Virginia)*

Cypress *(tree, Louisiana)*

Emerald *(gem, North Carolina)*

Dakota *(Sioux word for "friend")*

Galena *(mineral, Missouri)*

Holly *(tree, Delaware)*

Hope *(motto, Rhode Island)*

Iris *(flower, Tennessee)*

Jade *(gem, Wyoming)*
Jalapeno *(pepper, Texas)*
Kool-Aid *(drink, Nebraska)*
Kukui [pronounced *koo-koo-ee*] *(tree, Hawaii)*
Laurel *(flower, Connecticut)*
Lavender *(flower, Colorado)*
Lilac *(flower, New Hampshire)*
Lily *(flower, Utah)*
Magnolia *(flower, Mississippi)*
Morgan *(horse, Vermont)*
Niagara *(ship, Pennsylvania)*
Opal *(gem, Nevada)*
Palmetto *(tree, South Carolina)*
Pearl *(gem, Kentucky)*
Poppy *(flower, California)*
Robin *(bird, Michigan)*
Rose *(flower, Iowa)*
Sapphire *(gem, Montana)*
Scarlet *(flower, Ohio)*
Sitka *(tree, Alaska)*
Sunflower *(flower, Kansas)*
Syringa *(flower, Idaho)*
Tabby *(cat, Massachusetts)*
Trilobite *(fossil, Wisconsin)*
Tulip *(flower, Indiana)*

159

Turquoise *(gem, Arizona)*
Violet *(flower, New Jersey)*
Virginia *(It's a state!)*
Walleye *(fish, Minnesota)*
Willow *(bird, Washington)*
Wintergreen *(herb, Maine)*
Yucca *(flower, New Mexico)*

PLACE NAMES

Punkydoodles
Stonybatter
Takizawa
Bombay
Trinidad
Sopchoddy
Nimrod
Andorra
Ouagadougou [pronounced *wah-ga-doog-oo*]
Jamaica
Twitty
HooHoo
Katmandu
Flin Flon
Climpy

Yeehaw
Kyzyl [pronounced *ke-zil*]
Zonguldak
Samoa
Krypton
Woolloomooloo
Shanghai
Valtimo
Mashpee
Poopó
Odododiodoo
Lucia [pronounced *loo-chee-uh*]
Weedpatch
Doostil
Calabasas
Affpuddle
Pukë
Djibouti [pronounced *je-boot-ee*]
Bora Bora
Willacoochee
Kalamazoo
Glorioso
Vulcan
Mumbles
Wacahoota
Booti Booti

Zimbabwe
Meeteetse
Paducah
Wigtwizzle
Kyrgyzstan [pronounced *kir-je-stan*]
Coolmeelee
Piddlehinton
Weeki Wachee

Your Star Wars *Nickname*

Ever notice how all the characters in
Star Wars have similar futuristic names?
Here's how to get yours!

FOR YOUR STAR WARS FIRST NAME:

1. Take the first *three* letters of your
   last name.
2. Add to that, the first *two* letters of
   your first name.

FOR YOUR STAR WARS LAST NAME:

1. Take the first two letters of your
   mother's maiden name.

2. Add to that, the first three letters of the name of the city you were born in OR the street you live on now, whichever sounds better.

★ Want to make your last name seem classier? Add a "de" to the front of it, which in France shows that you have nobility in your family. Example: Kathy Blanchette can become Kathleen *de* Blanchette. Fancy!

★ Looking for a nice summer camp experience? Try visiting charming Lake Chargoggagoggmanchauggagoggchaubunagungamaugg in Massachusetts! It's the longest place name in the U.S. This name is pronounced just like it's spelled, like in the popular romantic song:

WE TOOK A WALK ONE NIGHT AND SAT ON A LOG

DOWN BY LAKE CHARGOGGAGOGGMAN-CHAUGGAGOGGCHAUBUNAGUNGAMAUGG

163

WE KISSED AND THEN WE HEARD A FROG

DOWN BY LAKE CHARGOGGAGOGGMAN-CHAUGGAGOGGCHAUBUNAGUNGAMAUGG

Everybody sing along!

Doodles

This is an addictive shape to draw. Once you follow these steps, it will be on the margins of all your papers!

In India, girls show their artistic ability by drawing *kolams*. These are simple yet

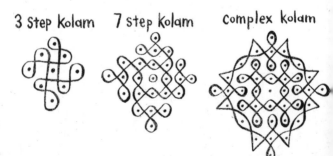

3 step kolam   7 step kolam   complex kolam

complex shapes that are supposed to bring good luck and health. The way to do it is simple. Just draw five dots across a page. Above and below it, put four dots in the spaces. Above and below those, put three dots, and so on.

Begin drawing one continuous loop that goes around ALL the dots. After you are done, you can decorate the doodle with symbols and pictures.

Name Quiz

See if you can get these questions about names right. The answers are at the bottom of page 166.

1. WHICH MONTH OF THE YEAR IS THE MOST POPULAR "MONTH" NAME FOR GIRLS?

2. WHAT IS THE ONLY STATE IN THE U.S. WITH A ONE-SYLLABLE NAME?

3. WHICH OF THESE NAMES WAS RECENTLY IN THE TOP TEN MOST POPULAR NAMES FOR GIRLS? BIMBERLY,

165

CRAYOLA, EBOLA, ELISABET, MOSSIE, PEPSI, PRUNELLA, ISABELLA, SALMONELLA, VELVEETA

4. MEGAN WRITES THE NAME OF A CERTAIN U.S. STATE ON A SHEET OF PAPER IN ALL CAPITAL LETTERS. SHE THEN TURNS THE PAGE UPSIDE DOWN AND LOOKS AT IT IN A MIRROR. THE REFLECTION READS EXACTLY THE SAME AS SHE WROTE IT. WHAT IS THE NAME OF THE STATE?

Answers below!

Handwriting

Every girl knows that one of the best ways to stay awake in a boring class is to practice signing her own name. There are so many possibilities; which one looks coolest? Which style reflects who you are?

This is what makes "calligraphy" [pronounced *kal-ig-raf-ee*] so interesting.

1. April 2. Maine 3. Isabella 4. OHIO

Calligraphy is the art of hand-writing beautiful letters and it can be done in different styles or fonts. Computers can be used for unique styles too, but learning to handwrite in a font is much more personal and artistic than pulling a paper out of the printer. And if you learn calligraphy, your notes in class will be admired by everyone!

Because handwriting is so personal, it's no surprise to us that the way we write can say something about us. Countries like Germany, Switzerland, and Israel put a lot of faith in handwriting. In France, people often must give handwriting samples for job applications. And in Israel, you may have your handwriting checked just to get an apartment!

The study of handwriting is called **graphology.** It is not scientific, but then, neither are hunches, intuition, or first impressions. Maybe because of this, most of the graphology experts in France are women.

You Be the Judge

If a person writes a few sentences or even a short paragraph on a blank sheet of paper, it can be analyzed. You could probably reach some conclusions yourself! For example, if a girl pushes down really hard with her pen when she writes, she is probably strong-willed and determined. But if she barely touches the paper with her pencil, it wouldn't be a surprise to find out she's shy.

Have a friend or family member give you a handwriting sample. Make sure to have the person sign her name at the bottom. (Don't say what the sample is for until *after* you've gotten it, though!) Then see what the handwriting reveals about your subject!

WHAT YOU SEE	WHAT IT MEANS
The letters are well-rounded.	This is a balanced person.
The letters are at straight angles.	This person has good energy and might be a leader.
There are little happy faces ☺, hearts ♥, or circles for the dot on the letter "i."	She has a unicorn collection.

WHAT YOU SEE	WHAT IT MEANS
The "a" or "o" letters are not all the way closed in.	The writer is talkative.
The "a" and "o" letters are closed in.	She can keep a secret.
There is a good space between the lines of the paragraph.	This is a stable person.
The letters *slant* to the right.	The writer has an energetic, passionate personality.
The letters *slant* to the left.	The person is timid and quiet.
It looks like the person wrote in a hurry, or it's just messy.	This shows an impatient person.
The lines of the words don't veer up or down.	She is a well-adjusted person.
The person prefers black ink.	This shows a strong personality.

170

WHAT YOU SEE	WHAT IT MEANS
The letters are small and maybe squished together.	She is shy and doesn't like attention. (Probably smart, too!)
There are big letters, or it's written in all capitals, or there are decorations on the letters.	These show a person who *likes attention.* She also doesn't like to be criticized. (So you may want to skip telling her this!)
There is a good-sized left margin.	The person is flexible and good at adapting.
The style of writing seems to change inside the paragraph.	This person gets bored easily and may be unreliable.
The right-hand margin is small.	She is friendly and open.

WHAT YOU SEE	WHAT IT MEANS
The cross on the letter "t" slants down. (Or up!)	If the bar slopes *down,* the person is a *rebel.* If it slants *up,* she has *high expectations* for herself and others.
There are big loops.	The person is a romantic, imaginative type.
The person has a complete, readable signature.	This shows maturity.

★ Teachers at a primary school in Smethwick, England, were ordered to always use green ink for correcting papers. Red ink is not allowed because it is too negative and might damage a student's self-esteem!

Secret Message Girl

If you don't know how to write in invisible ink yet, here's how to do it!

TECHNIQUE 1:

YOU WILL NEED: a white crayon, paper, a highlighter (any color but yellow).

If you write a message on *white* paper with a *white* crayon, it is nearly impossible to read. That is, it's nearly impossible until you run a highlighter over it! Then the letters shine right through. Try it and you'll see what we mean.

TECHNIQUE 2:

YOU WILL NEED: white paper, a small glass or jar, lemon juice, a cotton swab, a mirror.

First, pour the lemon juice into your glass. Lemony! Now just dip the cotton swab into the lemon juice and then use the swab to write your message on the paper. Re-dip the swab into the juice if it dries out while you're writing. (If you don't have lemon juice, milk also works for this technique.)

Let your writing dry out; it should become invisible. When you are ready to read the message, hold it up to a strong light or fire and the words will magically appear! Another way to get the message to appear is to have an adult use an iron at low temperature to "iron" the piece of paper. Because lemon juice (or milk) darkens when heated, the message shows up!

TECHNIQUE 3:

YOU WILL NEED: water, paper, two bowls, cornstarch, a chopstick (or any pen-shaped piece of wood), a sponge, and iodine (ask your mom if you have some in the house).

Pour ¼ cup of water into one of the bowls and stir 1 teaspoon of cornstarch into it. Pop it into the microwave for 30 to 40 seconds, stir it, and then microwave again for 30 to 40 seconds more. This is your ink!

Once it cools, take your chopstick, dip it into this mixture, and write your secret message on the paper. As the ink dries, it will become invisible.

Once the message dries, mix 8 to 9 drops of iodine with about ½ cup of water in another bowl. Take a sponge, dip it in this solution, and wring it out. Then gently sponge your paper with it. The invisible message will be magically revealed!

Bad Words

"FEAR OF A NAME INCREASES FEAR OF THE THING ITSELF." —J. K. Rowling

We guess it's no secret that jerks or mean girls sometimes use a word that rhymes with *witch*. (Just put a "b" where the "w" is.) The thing about "witch with a b" is that it just means an *adult female dog*. And most people like dogs! This word can also mean "to complain" when it is used as a verb. (There is a famous book

175

about knitting called *Stitch 'N Bitch*.) This word can also mean "a type of lamp used in Alaska." But many people only use the word's *slang* meaning, which is "a mean woman." Times change, and words change, too. Some women even consider this word a compliment to their strong personalities. (But you are not one of them.)

★ The word ***bitchin'*** can be used as an adjective for "good" or "cool."

Speaking of bad words, if a really mean boy ever tells you to go to h-e-[double hockey sticks], tell him you can't because your *passport* isn't ready. That's because there is a real village in Norway named Hell. People go there all the time! (And in the winter, when there are many cold days, it even freezes over.)

BTW, a school in Wellingborough, England, has a school policy that students are allowed to cuss up to five times per class period. Teachers are supposed to keep track of the cussing on the board.

Don't You Hate It When the Teacher Says ...

Here are some words you don't like to hear from your teacher:

No name, no credit.

Listen up, people!

Class average was a D-.

Don't raise your hand if you're going to forget what you were going to say.

Your homework is to have a good weekend.

I need to speak with you after class.

Let's keep it down to a dull roar.

You're going to regret not knowing this.

Pop quiz!

Lack of planning on your part does not create an emergency on my part.

If you take away MY time, I'll take away YOURS.

What are you eating? Did you bring enough for everyone?

Is that a note? ☹ *(Uh-oh!)*

"Allow the Mouth to Rejoice!"

The United Nations is a place where ALL the different nations on the planet come together to try and solve the world's problems. But since there are so many different languages spoken in the world, it's tough for everyone to know what is being said. Translators (people who are good at translating words from one language to another) get to work there.

The problem with translating from one language to another is that if you translate word for word, it won't make sense in the other language. For example, a U.N. translator once translated "Out of sight, out of mind" from English to Chinese. (This saying means "If you don't see it, you won't think about it.") In Chinese, the direct translation was "Invisible, insane." Not helpful! Translation mistakes like this happen all the time, and sometimes they are pretty funny.

"Uh..."

If you listen to people (or yourself) talk, you'll hear a LOT of "uh's" and "um's" (and even "er's"). People say "uh" and "um" to fill in space until they can think of the next word they are going to say. Because of this, these are called "filler words."

Men use filler words more than women do. This must be because girls are better at talking than boys, and so they don't need as much filler.

Another interesting thing is that not all cultures use the same filler words.

Here are some examples:

Hebrew: *ehhhhh*

Serbia and Croatia: *ovay*

Turkey: *mmmmmm*

Japan: *eto* [pronounced eh-to]

OR *ano* [pronounced ah-no]

Spain: *este*

Mandarin Chinese: *jiege* [pronounced JEH-guh]

France: *euh*

Sweden: *eh, ah, aah, hmmm, ooh, oh*

Both Pepsi and Coca-Cola have had problems translating their ads into Chinese. Pepsi wanted to have the slogan *Come alive with the Pepsi generation!* put on billboards in China, but when they did this, they ran into trouble. That's because the translator had written *Pepsi brings back your dead ancestors* as the new motto!

Coca-Cola's translation problems were even worse. When Coke started to sell its product in China, shopkeepers began making signs to advertise the product. Trying to spell *Coca-Cola* in Chinese resulted in many mistakes; one of them was *Bite the wax tadpole.*

Coca-Cola quickly had a new motto written, which translated to *Allow the mouth to rejoice.*

When Coors translated their ad motto *Turn It Loose!* into Spanish, it became *Suéltalo con Coors,* which can mean the same as *Get diarrhea from Coors.* Yech!

181

We don't think that's the message they wanted to send. And when Clairol tried to shop their new curling iron (called the Mist Stick) in Germany, it didn't sell well. Someone finally pointed out that in German slang *mist* means *manure*. Who wants a manure stick in their hair? Nobody!

Beauty

"BEAUTY IS IN THE EYE OF THE BEHOLDER, AND IT MAY BE NECESSARY FROM TIME TO TIME TO GIVE A STUPID OR MISINFORMED BEHOLDER A BLACK EYE." — *Miss Piggy*

In the animal kingdom, the boys are usually the flashy show-offs; you know, like with lions, peacocks, hamsters, that sort of thing. But we humans reverse this trend, and girls tend to be the ones wearing more jewelry, makeup, and more interesting clothing than boys.

But what IS beautiful? If you have ever traveled to another country, you know that what one culture thinks is **beautiful,** another culture might consider just **weird.** Every society has "rules" for what is beautiful. So there has to be more than just ONE way to be beautiful. And what you think is good-looking is probably what you have been taught is good-looking by our society!

Even more confusing is the fact that the "rules" for beauty **always** change. Fifty years ago, Miss America was supposed to be the most beautiful woman in the United States. But compared to the Miss America today, she would be considered short and overweight. What happened? *The rules changed!*

Of course, having rules for beauty is stupid. Anyone can be beautiful in almost any way that you can imagine. Sometimes the thing that makes a girl beautiful is a strong nose or a slanted smile. Because the girl doesn't look *perfect,* THAT is the interesting thing about her. The French even have a term for this sort of beauty: *jolie laide* [pronounced *zjo-lee led*]. Like the writer Mavis Jukes says, "You don't have to be pretty to be beautiful."

"ENERGY IS MORE ATTRACTIVE THAN BEAUTY." *—Louisa May Alcott*

★ In 2004, an Ohio woman caught stealing $1 million in diamonds told police officers she was too "cute" to go to jail. (She was sentenced to three years.)

Here's "Beauty Logic" for you: If there is something about you that you think is beautiful (like your hair!), you can't ever say so. People would think you were *stuck-up!* But if there is something about your appearance that you *don't* like, it's perfectly okay to obsess about it and complain about it to your friends. They practically expect it. Weird, huh?

It's all in the way we see ourselves. In France, 80 percent of people look carefully at themselves in a mirror at least once a day. While 88 percent of French men like what they see, only 73 percent of French women think they look good. (And only 1 percent of French women think they are beautiful!) That's odd because most people think that women are *more* attractive to look at than men. After all, if you look at the covers of women's magazines, *women* are on the cover. If you look at the covers of a lot of men's magazines, *women* are on the cover too!

★ *GOOD NEWS!* Research suggests that most people think that the face of a 12- to 14-year-old girl is one of the most appealing faces around. Whoo-hoo!

The sad fact is that people have always been judged by the way they look. In order to test yourself to see if this beauty peer pressure has gotten to you, try the following activity:

Walk by a Mirror ... and Don't Look!

This is hard for anyone to do.... Try it for a day and you'll see why!

YOU WILL NEED: Reflective surfaces.

In the course of a day, you will walk by many surfaces that reflect your image . . . mirrors, windows, mirrors, newly washed cars, mirrors, and mirrors. The natural reaction that women and men have is to look at themselves when they get a chance.

Try starting off your day with *one* good look in the mirror as you get ready for school. Then DON'T look at yourself again until noon. (Just check to make sure that there's nothing in your teeth. That's it!) If you can restrain yourself from looking at yourself the rest of the day, you are probably not too self-conscious!

★ Practice checking yourself in the mirror really fast—check your nose and teeth for trouble and move on.

Boys are as bad about this as girls. Find a spot where there is a big reflective window and watch boys and men walk past it. Although some will walk right by, many will "check themselves out."

Beauty Is Only Skin Deep

"WHEN I WAS YOUR AGE . . . I WISH I'D KNOWN THAT I ALREADY HAD EVERY-THING I NEEDED WITHIN MYSELF TO BE HAPPY, INSTEAD OF LOOKING FOR HAPPINESS AT BEAUTY COUNTERS."
—Ilene Beckerman

Many children's stories have a moral like "Beauty is only skin deep." We're not so sure about that. How much deeper should it go? Who wants cute kidneys? We've also read stories with a moral like "true beauty is on the inside." What good is that? Nobody will ever see it!

It's nice to know that some people think that beauty is as much about *brains and personality* as appearances. In Russia, the people got to vote for their 2004 Miss Universe. The winner by a huge margin was a 14-year-old girl named Alyona. She wore a T-shirt and didn't put on any makeup. One of the Russians who voted for Alyona did so because she disliked "unnatural beauties who cannot be distinguished from each other with their fake emotions and smiles." Wow! Unfortunately Alyona was disqualified because she was too young. ***Dang it!***

It's time to take a special tour of beauty's SECRETS, HISTORIES, and MYSTERIES!

Can You Say "Trout Pout"?

Ever wonder why your lips are a different color than the rest of you? It's because there are a lot more little veins (called *capillaries*) under the skin of your lips than there are underneath your regular skin. (If you've ever cut your lip, that's why it bleeds so much.) You can tell someone is sick if her lips are pale; this shows bad blood circulation!

The most common cosmetics that go on the mouth are lipstick, lip gloss, and lip liner. But adding *color* isn't the only way that women have beautified their lips. They've also done "lip exercises." It was once thought that pronouncing words with a lot of "Ps" would give lips a good workout and make them fuller. Girls used to walk around talking about "popcorn and pumpkins" to get puffy lips. Some girls even did lip weightlifting. You've heard of push-ups and pull-ups, but how about lip-ups?

But before you think how weird that is, keep in mind that many girls and women in the United States today buy *lip plumpers,* which irritate and sting lips so that they get puffy. These plumpers use things like cayenne powder or cinnamon oil to do their stinging. Ouch! Girls who lip plump too much suffer from "trout pout." Their lips start looking like a fish face!

★ The Japanese used to think it was rude to show someone your open mouth, which is why many Japanese women cover their mouths when laughing even today.

Expressions

Our face can communicate how we are feeling more quickly than words. Our *expressions* EXPRESS our feelings! And because we are complicated, our expressions can communicate complicated feelings instead of just one at a time. In other words, someone can smile sadly, even though these are two different emotions.

Computers using emotion-recognition software can be used to analyze these feelings. One such computer was used to look at the Mona Lisa's famous smile. The computer found that the smile was 83 percent happy, 9 percent disgusted, 6 percent afraid, and 2 percent angry. Since Leonardo da Vinci painted her, you could say that we now know the Da Vinci Code!

The Eyes Have It

Eyes are usually the first thing someone sees when they look at you. But even though we "beautify" our eyelids, eyebrows, and eyelashes, we usually leave our eye*balls* alone. Most eye makeup makes the eyebrows and eyelashes darker. The ancient Egyptians called eye makeup *kohl,* and it had a practical purpose. *Kohl* was used to protect eyes from the desert sun. You may have seen football players with black streaked beneath their eyes for the same reason. Cleopatra put blue-black kohl on her upper eyelids and green on her *lower* lids.

To get the perfect eye makeup mix, Egyptians mixed either honey, crocodile poop, and onion water OR ground donkey liver, oil, and opium. ***Gross!*** BTW, nowadays, there is clear mascara, which is terrific for separating lashes. (It can also be used as an "eyebrow gel" to keep your brows looking good!)

As for eyebrows, American girls didn't start tweezing (or even shaving) their eyebrows until the 1920s. Tweezing has continued right up until today. Not only that, but men are getting in on the act as well. Recently, a growing number of men have also begun to have their eyebrows "shaped" with plucking and waxing. (This is called *manscaping*.)

If you're going to tweeze your eyebrows, try to keep them looking **natural!** For some reason, there are girls who get a little crazy with the tweezers and they start pulling everything in sight. This is painful and silly, especially when they end up using eyebrow pencils to fill in the holes where their hair was.

Although it's not such a big deal anymore, pierced eyebrows used to be a real "in your face" way of getting people to pay attention. (Get it? "In your face"?) But eyebrow piercings can be dangerous, because they can damage nerves and leave part of a person's face numb.

*"THE THING YOU HATE ABOUT YOUR-
SELF TENDS TO BE THE THING THAT
EVERYONE LIKES ABOUT YOU."*
—Nicole Kidman

Do You Pick Your Nose?

If you "pick your nose" as the best part of
your face, you're not alone. Native Americans like the Nez Perce (which means
"Pierced Nose") used piercings to draw
attention to the center of the face. Women
in Pakistan and India have worn delicate
nose ornaments for centuries. Sometimes
a fine chain will lead from a woman's nose
to a hair ornament or earring. And the
ancient Romans believed that a strong,
assertive nose was a sign of intelligence
and leadership ability.

Do Your Ears Hang Low?

As for ears, they might be the most
ignored part of the face. **How unfair!**

This isn't a face "rule," but a doctor told us that most people have ears that are about as long as their nose. Check to see if this is true for you!

Do you have earlobes? (This is the lower part of your ear that may hang down a bit.) A traditional Buddhist belief is that long earlobes are a sign of great wisdom. And long earlobes are thought to be beautiful for members of the Kelabit tribe of Borneo. Women there stretch their earlobes so that they hang anywhere from two to eight inches down from their head! At that length, they can tickle your shoulders. (That reminds us of a song: ***Do your ears hang low? Do they wobble to and fro? Can you tie 'em in a knot . . .*** Okay, we'll stop now.)

Getting pierced ears is pretty common for U.S. girls. You should know that studies show that if the ear piercing goes through cartilage (in the stiffer part of the ear), the chances for infection are greatly increased. One study found an infection rate of almost 30 percent for cartilage piercings. Yikes!

★ In traditional Japanese culture, pierced ears are considered bad luck.

In Your Face!

"YOUR BRAIN IS THE MOST IMPORTANT PART OF YOUR BODY. THAT'S BECAUSE GOOD LOOKS COME AND GO, BUT YOUR BRAIN WILL ALWAYS BE THERE."
—*Sarah Nader*

In India, the *forehead* is believed to be one of the most important parts of the body. Indian women sometimes have a red or yellow mark in the middle of the forehead called a *tilak* or a *bindi*. The *tilak* is a sign of good fortune; it shows that the person wearing it is pure and thoughtful. The decoration is also supposed to keep the mind calm. Although the *tilak* may show that the woman wearing it is married, it can also be a fashion accessory. (Young

197

girls wearing the *tilak* usually have it done in a light red color.)

Fun and Natural Facials

It's time for a guacamole facial! It's fun AND natural! Just cut an avocado in half and remove the pit and peel. Mash up the avocado. Then smear it on your face! Leave it on for around five minutes and then wash it off with warm water. The natural oils from the avocado will soften and moisturize your face.

The egg white facial is another natural beautifier. You need one egg for this. Crack it, remove the yolk, and whip up

The Bigger, the Better!

For originality, you've got to like the standard of beauty that the Massa have. The Massa is a tribe of Africans who live in Chad. For them, the bigger, the *better*. The most beautiful feature a woman can have is rolls of fat on her neck!

the whites in a small bowl. Then spread it on your face. Once you've done so, lie down for a while and let it dry. Then wash and wipe your face clean.

Trim and Polish

You've probably noticed that your fingernails grow faster than your toenails. Most fingernails grow about an inch and a half a year, while toenails grow just half an inch. (This is because your hands have better blood circulation than your feet, and they get more nutrients.)

★ Psychologists believe that fingernail and cuticle biters may be more stubborn than most people.

To decorate their nails, girls in the United States started using nail polish in the 1920s. For a long time, pink was the only color considered "appropriate." If a girl painted her nails red, she was considered a troublemaker!

You might be surprised to learn that "manicures" and "pedicures" don't actually *cure* anything. Nope; this is simply what we call **trimming** and **polishing** fingernails and toenails. They are also a terrific way to "pamper" yourself. It turns out that getting your nails soaked, buffed, polished, finished, filed, decorated, and colored feels pretty good. And it's also a fun thing to do with a friend! Massage her hands with lotion, and to keep her nails soft, wrap them in warm, wet towels. Use a clipper and nail file to shape her nails. *Note:* You may want to take a bath or soak your toes in warm water for five to ten minutes before going through the above steps for a pedicure.

When done, it's time to paint or polish! Clear polish is the most natural look, but if you want to do some color painting, most girls try to match whatever color lipstick they might be wearing. If you're in a creative mood, you could paint each nail in a different color. You can also put clear nail polish on a fingernail and then sprinkle glitter on it. After it's dry, just put one more layer of clear polish on, and you have glitter nails!

★ If you ever want to whiten your fingernails, try sticking them into a cut piece of lemon for a while. (Make sure you don't have any fingernail cuts before you do this . . . ouch!)

★ *HOT TIP!* If there is a beauty school near you, they probably offer manicures and pedicures for way cheap.

★ *FUN NAIL TRICK:* Try putting scratch 'n' sniff stickers on your fingernails. They're nontoxic and will make your fingernails smell good all day!

PRACTICAL JOKE ALERT! We encourage you to sneak up on your brother or father while he's asleep and paint as many of his finger and/or toenails as you can reach. Once the painted man wakes up, try to rush him off to work or school as fast as possible so that he doesn't notice!

I'll Never Look Like Her

"WHO I AM INSIDE DETERMINES HOW I FEEL ABOUT MY BODY, NOT THE OTHER WAY AROUND." —Alanis Morissette

In ancient Greece, girls were supposed to be *slim* and *trim*. In order to get their daughters beautiful, Greek mothers sometimes wrapped up their baby daughters tightly with fabric for the first months of their lives to squish and lengthen them. (Sort of a **Play-Doh Not-So-Fun Factory of Beauty** for real girls!)

If that seems weird to you, think about this: The average American woman is about 5' 4" tall and weighs around 150 pounds. The average American fashion model is about 5' 10" tall and weighs around 115 pounds. There are 3.5 billion women in the world, and only a few thousand of them are models. And even *models* don't look like models. What if you took away the airbrushing, makeup, and expensive clothes?

Anyway, think about who you are comparing yourself to. Are you putting yourself through a *Play-Doh Not-So-Fun Factory of Beauty* to look like something you're not? Other countries have beliefs about the female body that can be the opposite of U.S. culture. For example, in the United States, girls sometimes get eating disorders trying to keep their weight *down.* In the West African country of Mauritania, overweight women have long been thought of as attractive. They have problems with girls eating too *much!* Fortunately, the United States and Mauritania are both trying to educate girls about proper nutrition.

It is possible that times might be slowly changing. Mannequins are sort of like store "models," and lately some of them have been made with 38-inch hips, which is much bigger than they used to be. Storeowners say they now have "butts with attitude" which are easier to model jeans on realistically. ☺

The Belly Button

It's so cute, and so important! In Japan, the belly has long been believed to be a source of a person's warmth and vitality. Traditional Japanese women's clothing has a wide cloth belt around the midsection to protect the belly and keep it warm. The Japanese believe that the perfect belly button (or navel) is narrow, vertical . . . and an "innie"!

As cute as it is, your belly button is also your first *scar*. It is the scar tissue left over from when the doctor cut the umbilical cord that connected you to your mom. So that means some girls show off their scars with short blouses and tops. It's weird to think about the belly button that way!

★ Belly button experts have not been able to figure out why belly button lint is almost always blue, even if it comes from a girl who owns no blue clothing.

In the United States, girls generally have to be 18 to get their belly buttons pierced. (It is one of the slowest-healing piercings there is.) If you want to have a little fun, try the following practical joke.

Fake Belly-Button Piercing

It's time for a fake belly-button piercing. (This trick also works for a fake nose piercing.)

YOU WILL NEED: Beads, glue, a belly button or nose.

Stop by a bead store and look for a bead that you can use to get a "piercing." For a nose piercing, find a small bead with a flat back. If you want a custom belly-button piercing, you may want to get a larger, more impressive bead, maybe even one you could attach a small chain to.

This trick is best done after you have been out of the house for a while. Wait until it's almost time to return home, and then put a little dab of white Elmer's glue (not Krazy Glue!) on the back of the bead. Hold it against your nostril or belly. Be patient and keep it there in place until the glue dries.

Then you're ready to parade into the house! Act like you're sort of guilty and trying to hide it, but make sure it's visible, too. Then watch your mom shriek and your dad yell before you tell them, "Just kidding!"

Getting Soggy in the Tub

Have you ever noticed how your fingers shrivel up when you stay in the bathtub too long? (And then you can pretend you're an old lady!) Guess what? Your fingers don't actually shrivel. The skin just gets BIGGER.

What happens is that the longer you stay in the water, the more water molecules soak into your skin tissue. This stretches the skin out. Basically, you're getting soggy! And the younger you are, the further your skin stretches in the tub.

Beautiful Skin

"IF YOU TAKE GOOD CARE OF YOUR SKIN, YOU WON'T NEED MUCH MAKEUP."
—*Brooke Vermillion*

Dr. Ellen Gendler is a skin-care expert who was asked the all-important question: "What is the most common skin care mistake girls make?" Her answer: "Picking at their pimples or using too much moisturizer." Okay, good to know!

Can you believe that *freckles* were once thought to be a sign of disease? Naturally, there were cures for this horrible condition, like having a girl rinse her face with dew and then saying the alphabet backward.

In India, the people have a cool tradition of skin painting. A plant called "henna" grows in India, the Middle East, and northern Africa. It provides leaves that can be used for a safe dye, usually in some shade of red. The temporary dye can be used for body painting or "mehndi." Women have patterns painted on their hands, feet, or entire bodies, especially for special occasions like marriages. And a new bride didn't have to do any housework until her wedding mehndi wore off. (See pages 131–134 in **"Fun Stuff to Do"** to learn how to paint with henna.)

Although almost nobody has pure white skin, this hasn't stopped women from trying to get it with makeup. In the past, Japanese women used face powder made from rice, which was organic and nontoxic. In Europe, some Englishwomen wanted white faces so badly, they put leeches behind their ears to literally suck the blood out of their heads. **Gross!**

In modern times, many people think tans are cool, but of course, tanning can create skin problems. Girls with light skin and light eyes are the most at risk for skin cancer and should be the most careful about becoming a *tanorexic.* A *tanorexic* is someone who thinks that she's too pale, even when she is *really tan.* The thing is, tans always wear off anyway, but skin cancer can stick around for a long time.

★ *UNAPPEALING PEELING!* When skin peels off after a bad sunburn, it is called *blype.* Now you know.

Goose Bumps!

When you get cold, your skin often gets little bumps on it, which are called goose bumps or goose pimples. How did they get such a weird name?

The little feathers called "goose down" are useful for stuffing pillows and comforters. These obviously came from geese, and some geese get their down feathers plucked as many as five times a year. Once the goose has its feathers plucked, it gets cold and is covered in goose bumps or goose pimples. What happens is that the goose has small muscles surrounding each feather, which raises the feather up or down depending on the temperature. When it's cold, a goose will "puff up" its feathers to create warmth. Without any feathers, the naked goose just gets covered with little bumps of muscles trying to move feathers that aren't there. Sad!

Humans work under the same system. We don't have feathers, but we do have hair.

Even though there isn't much of it, when it's cold, our skin muscles try to raise up our hairs to create warmth for ourselves. We can also get goose bumps when we are frightened. Then it is called *horripilation*. Even though these goose bumps are scary, experts like Stephen King agree that *horripilation* is harmless.

Perfume

Smells can have an influence on how we feel. Some people get headaches if they smell something bad, and some people believe that good smells can help us feel better and stay healthy. This is called *aromatherapy.* In aromatherapy, some plant oils, including essential oils, are thought to have the following effects:

Rose, chamomile, and **lavender** increase feelings of calmness and well-being.

Jasmine, orange, and **cypress** increase feelings of confidence.

Geranium, grapefruit, and **sandalwood** are used to treat depression.

Basil, frankincense, and **peppermint** are used to help with low energy.

Black pepper, basil, and **rosemary** improve memory and concentration.

★ In traditional Japanese society, women put their clothes in small, enclosed spaces and burned incense with them so the clothing would smell good.

Nowadays, many perfumes smell somewhat similar because they have an alcohol base. (That's why they evaporate so fast.) If you're looking for a perfume that doesn't smell like everyone else's, there's a store in Williamsburg, Virginia, for you. It specializes in very particular smells, including a ripe tomato, moist earth, fir trees, or roast beef. Believe it or not, there are even more specialized and unusual bottled odors for sale, like Play-Doh and Doll Head (the smell of the vinyl head of a doll!). How *scentsible* is that?

Sadly, the quest for pricey perfume can have bad impacts on the natural world. For example, the Brazilian rosewood tree once peacefully grew in the wilds of the Amazon. When the perfume called Chanel No. 5 came out in 1921, that all changed. Chanel No. 5 uses rosewood oil, and soon the oil was being used in other perfumes, soaps, and scented candles. Today, the rosewood tree is an endangered species.

Make Your Own Perfumed Body Scrub

You can make your own perfumed scrub without destroying any species.

YOU WILL NEED: A wide-mouthed glass jar with a lid you can clamp or screw down, kosher salt, olive oil, an essential oil you like the smell of (like lemon, eucalyptus, rose, or peppermint), and cinnamon.

Fill your jar a little less than halfway up with kosher salt. Then pour almost as much olive oil into the jar and start mixing until it feels right to you.

Next add in four drops of your essential oils and a tablespoon of cinnamon! Mix it all up completely. (There are no rules, so if you want to throw in some lemon zest, rosemary, or flower petals, go ahead!) Then let it sit for a while.

When you're ready to use it, just bring the jar with you into the shower. Take a scoop of the scrub out and rub it on your joints and your feet. Be sure to rinse it all off, and don't slip on the oily mix while you're in there! (Don't put your *body* scrub on your face, either. It's not designed for it, and it's probably illegal where you live.)

★ *HOT TIP!* Here's our hot tip with perfume: **A little bit goes a long way.** We're sure you've noticed the boy who puts on half a bottle of cologne after P.E. class at school. He reeks! He thinks that since a little cologne smells good, a *lot* smells great. You know how wrong he is, so don't make the exact same mistake.

Makeup

"BEAUTY, TO ME, IS ABOUT BEING COMFORTABLE IN YOUR OWN SKIN. THAT, OR A KICK-ASS RED LIPSTICK."
—*Gwyneth Paltrow*

MAKE UP means "to invent." So does that mean if you wear makeup you are trying to *invent* a new face for yourself, one that isn't yours? Maybe that's why some people call it *fake-up!* Women who always wear makeup sometimes say they feel "naked" without it on. So are women improving their faces with cosmetics or are they using it to hide behind?

Many people have struggled with this question. In Alexandria, Egypt, it was once illegal for unmarried women to wear makeup because the men were worried that they would be tricked into marrying someone who wasn't who she seemed to be. And nowadays, girls often argue with their parents about wearing makeup. Sometimes these arguments go all the way to a court of law. In Los Angeles, a judge once banned a Mexican-American girl from using makeup against her parents' wishes.

As far as cosmetics go, listen to your parents and "make up" your own mind. Just don't let yourself become your own favorite hobby or after-school project. Then you really will be stuck on yourself!

Most teenage girls in the U.S. do use makeup of some kind. There are bazillions of books and magazines out there with beauty tips about when you can wear purple eyeshadow (*never!*) or how to paint your toenails. You probably know more tips, tricks, ideas, and cool stuff than we do, but for those of you just barely getting into makeup, here are some of the basics.

Makeup Basics

If you are applying makeup to your skin and then cleaning it off again day after day, it's actually pretty hard on your skin. So maybe the most important tip is this: Don't use too much makeup! Experts agree that this is the most common mistake that girls make. (Of course, you don't need experts to tell you that; you've probably seen these mistakes at school!)

★ In France, girls and women try NOT to look as if they are spending hours on their faces. French girls favor makeup that is so natural, you don't notice it's there. The key is not to try too hard. If you *can* see obvious makeup on a woman's face, the French have a word for it: ***vulgaire*** (vulgar).

★ *BASIC SAFETY!* Don't share cosmetics with your friends. Be sure to wash makeup off before going to sleep at night. (Leaving it on for too long is bad for your skin.) Oh, and never keep cosmetics for more than six months. After that, they may have germs living in them. Ick!

BASE MAKEUP/FOUNDATION: The idea of base makeup (or "foundation") is to make your skin look like it doesn't have any blemishes or look too shiny. So it's important that the base you choose matches your skin type. Experiment with different shades till you get one that's just right.

Tip: Blend, blend, blend! Your face should not be a different color than your neck. And try not to overdo it. Some people call this "pancake" makeup, and it's not usually a good thing to have your face compared to breakfast food.

CONCEALER: This is a thick makeup that is good for hiding really bad blemishes . . . okay, pimples. Like your base, make sure it matches your skin. *Tip:* Try dabbing it on, instead of spreading it on. That way, it's less noticeable.

EYELINER: Your eyelids are one of the most sensitive parts of your body, so be very careful using application wands with eye liners and mascara. (And never put on eye makeup in a moving car!) Apply the eyeliner outside of the lash line, away from the eye. *Tip:* Don't overdo it, or you'll have raccoon eyes.

EYE SHADOW: The basic idea of eye shadow is that if you wear lighter shades of it, it will make your eyes appear bigger. Darker shades will make your eyes appear some-what smaller. ***Tip:*** Remember, nobody has naturally purple eyelids unless they've been hit in a boxing match!

MASCARA: Don't keep mascara for more than three months. If you're going to use an eyelash curler, use it before you put on your mascara! And although water-proof mascara won't "streak," some girls' eyes get irritated by it. Also, water-based mascara is much easier to remove. ***Tip:*** If your mascara gives you "tarantula eyelashes," you're overdoing it.

BLUSH: By highlighting cheeks with a rosy color, a girl can look like she just exer-cised. How healthy! Either that, or like she's blushing from embarrassment. ***Tip:*** Gel blushes are more difficult to apply than powder or cream blushes.

LIP LINER: If you can't really tell where your lips end and your skin begins, then lip liners are handy. They also make a nice outline around your lips so your lipstick doesn't "bleed" out past your lips onto your skin. If you want to use a lip liner, make a border around your lips, and then use lipstick or lip gloss inside the line. Fun!

LIP GLOSS, LIPSTICK: Do you want your lips to look "wetter" or more colorful? These are the difficult questions. Lipstick can also make lips look a bit bigger than they are, but be sure not to use it beyond the edges of your lips. ***Tip:*** Don't choose a lipstick color that is so bright, hummingbirds are attracted to your face.

PAINTING FINGERNAILS AND TOENAILS: Before painting fingernails or toenails, make sure that you wash them very well. Then trim and file them down. Once you start painting, use short, even strokes going in the same direction. When you're done, dip a cotton swab in polish remover and carefully remove any excess polish around your nails. (Some girls also like to put cotton balls between their toes when painting them, just to be safe.)

Tip: Both fingernail polish remover and some nail polishes are FLAMMABLE, so be careful. No burning candles when painting nails!

PETROLEUM JELLY may be the best makeup that isn't makeup. It can be used as a lip gloss or to make eyelashes and eyebrows look glossy. A little bit rubbed into each cheek gives the skin moisture and color.

Hair

"WOW, BLOSSOM, IT'S AMAZING HOW SILKY YOUR HAIR IS, CONSIDERING IT SMELLS SO FUNKY." —*The Powerpuff Girls*

There are **four** parts of your body that are not actually alive. See if you can guess what *one* of them is! (Are you guessing? This is a pretty hard one!)

That's right, your *hair* is not alive![1] Your

---

1. *If we count your hair and nails as one category (they're both made with keratin), the other nonliving parts of your body are your cartilage, tendons, and the solid part of your bones.*

hair is made up of the same stuff that makes fingernails, feathers, and hooves. It's a protein called *keratin*. But you sure can do a LOT with it. A little rearranging with a hairclip, or a lot of styling with a haircut and dye can change a girl's look dramatically. And it's so easy! All you have to do is shampoo, condition, rinse, dry, pluck, shave, cut, dye, perm, style, bleach, curl or relax, crimp, braid, comb and brush your hair and it's good to go!

Hair has long been thought to have special powers. People in many cultures saved and destroyed their hair clippings so that their enemies couldn't use their hair to cast spells against them. Julius Caesar shaved the heads of his enemies to teach them the power of ancient Rome. And today, some Jews and Muslims feel that for a woman to be properly modest, her hair should be covered when she is out in public.

★ Two thousand years ago, Jewish law allowed a man to divorce his wife by uncovering her hair.

We humans have the longest hair of all the animals. Without haircuts, the hairs on your head could get up to four feet long or more. A man named Tray Van Hay has the longest hair in the world. He has not had a haircut in over 30 years, and he's grown his hair over 20 feet long. The *good news* is that if there was a fire on the second floor of a building, you could use his hair as a way of escape. The *bad news?* Tray Van Hay hasn't washed his hair in six years! Talk about oily . . .

★ If you added up the hair growth of ALL of your hair over your lifetime, it comes to about 590 miles.

If you've ever had a haircut and then noticed that your hair took *forever* to grow out, it was probably taking a *growing break.* Hair grows in a cycle of anywhere between 2 to 7 years, and then it takes it easy for a few months before kicking in again with more growth. And the average human hair lives between 6 to 10 years, and then it goes dormant and falls out.

You lose 50 to 100 hairs a day because of this, but new hairs grow in their place.

★ If your dad doesn't have any hair, tell him he's not bald, he's *glabrous*. That should make him feel better!

The Ups and Downs of Having . . .

RED HAIR: Because only 2 percent of people in the United States have *naturally* red hair, redheads probably get more attention. That's nice if you *like* attention, and redheads have been getting more than their fair share for a long time. Many ancient Romans thought that red hair on a woman was the most attractive color there was. It's so special, fairies and pixies in stories and art are usually depicted with red hair.

★ In the United Kingdom (where 10 percent of people have red hair), redheads are called "coppertops" and red hair is often called "ginger hair."

The downside of being a redhead is that red is a symbol of fire, blood, passion, and anger. This has created a stereotype that redheads are hot-tempered and out-of-control. Ancient Egyptians considered redheads to be so "special" they were treated as foreigners. Modern people will ask redheads if their hair color is real and kids may call them "carrot top." (And don't forget the annoying boy who whispers, "I see RED people!")

★ Interesting fact! Studies show that redheads, especially women, may not be as sensitive to pain as other people.

REALLY CURLY HAIR: Really curly hair can be any color, but it is often black. Girls with really curly hair can wear it in an *afro,* a *semi-fro* (almost an afro) or a *low-fro* (a really short afro). Interestingly, girls with *straight* hair often want *curly* hair, while girls with *curly* hair sometimes wish

their hair were *straight*. So if a curly-haired girl gets a "permanent," she has her hair "relaxed" or "conked" (straightened), and if a girl with straight hair gets a "permanent," she gets her hair all curly. Funny, huh?

Really curly hair has unique style possibilities. For instance, it is perfect to braid with. Curly hair can be turned into a tight *cornrow* (braided close to the scalp.) In Nigeria, members of the Igbo tribe braid their hair tight to the head and end up with geometric patterns laid out on their heads. Curly hair can also be grown into dreadlocks more easily than any other hair type. **Dreadlocks** are what happen when you don't comb long curly hair; it can then be easily twisted into "natural" looking braids.

★ Many African American women (and men) grew their afros out in the 1960s to show their African roots. Today, it is estimated that about 70 percent of black women have their hair straightened or "conked."

BLONDE HAIR: There are more clichés about girls with blonde hair than any other hair color. Because many babies are born blonde (and then their hair darkens as they get older), blonde hair is associated with *innocence,* but not *intelligence.* Our culture says that *Blondes have more fun,* but women with this hair color are also sometimes referred to as *dumb blondes*. (Just so you know, scientists agree that hair color has nothing to do with intelligence!)

★ Marilyn Monroe was an actress from the twentieth century. She was famous for being the source of the stereotype of the dumb blonde. Guess what? She was a brunette!

Blonde hair was thought of as "good" in places like Greece and Italy. After all, Aphrodite (a.k.a. Venus), the goddess of love, was a blonde. Also, because most Greek and Italian women have dark hair, blondes were rare and considered special. Black haired women sometimes rubbed yellow mud and saffron (an orange-yellow dye) into their scalps to look blonde. (If you've ever wondered how many women in the United States are natural blondes, the answer is only about 5 to 15 percent of them.)

★ Blondes sometimes get a rare condition called loose anagen syndrome.

This means they have hair that can be pulled out very easily; just combing it is enough to pull the hair out. Luckily, the hairs usually toughen up as the girl gets older.

BROWN HAIR: **Brunettes Are Number One!** Brown is the most common hair color for humans. And there are probably more variations of brown hair than any other color. For example, girls can have brown hair that is so dark it looks black. Or a brunette can have auburn or mahogany hair, which is brown hair with red highlights.

Brown hair is thought of as being natural and earthy, and it looks great in the sunlight. Brunettes may also be taken more seriously by other people. If a brunette has light brown hair that is almost blonde in color, some people call this "dishwater blonde," "dirty blonde," or "swamp-water blonde." (Some people are apparently messed up!)

★ *BAD HAIR JOKE ALERT:*
Q. What do you call a brunette in a roomful of blondes?
A. Invisible.

BLACK HAIR: Dark hair is beautiful; it has a mystery and magic all its own. It can be anything from a very dark brown to jet-black, like many Asian, Latin, and black women have. Cleopatra, one of the world's most famous enchantresses, almost certainly had black hair. In Mexico, the women of the Tzotzil people pull black hair from their combs and save it. They believe that after death they can climb to paradise on a rope of their own hair. And *Chicanas* in the Mexican-American community have a hair fashion that involves really long hair with lots of body, curls, and flips.

BONUS! BLACK HAIR HAS THE BEST WORDS TO DESCRIBE IT. FOR EXAMPLE: ebony, inky, glossy, sable, lustrous, jet, or blue-black.

LONG HAIR: Long hair looks cool, and it's good for getting attention. When a long-haired girl swings her mane around or runs her hands through her hair, people can't help but notice. (And from Samson to the kings of France, men have thought that long hair gave them strength.) Although it's a lot of work to take care of, long hair can also symbolize freedom. In many traditional societies, a girl would wear her hair in a long braid. Once she was married, she would wind the braid into a bun at the back of her neck.

SHORT HAIR: We'll keep this short. ☺ There are three important things to say about short hair:

1. *IT'S USUALLY EASIER TO TAKE CARE OF THAN LONG HAIR.*

2. *PEOPLE TEND TO TAKE WOMEN WITH SHORT HAIR MORE SERIOUSLY.*

3. *IT'S STILL FEMININE!*

HAIR WEAVES: Braiding, extending, or weaving with colored silk, thread, or another person's hairs can really change a girl's look. The women of the Hmong tribe of Southeast Asia may take the prize for most variety with their hair extensions. They use cotton, hemp, and black wool and weave it into huge combs stuck into their hair.

★ About one-quarter of black women use weaves, extensions, or "additions."

BLEACHED HAIR: Oh no! You were the victim of a horrible laundry accident. ☺

★ *UNCOMB-ABLE HAIR:* Uncomb-able hair syndrome is a medical condition where a girl (or boy) has hair that literally CANNOT BE COMBED! (Don't worry, if you don't have this condition by now, you never will.) People with this condition (also called *cheveux incoiffables*) have hair that stands straight up. You can gel it all you want, and it won't matter. This hair is literally impossible to work with.

BAD HAIR: If you suffer from "bad hair," or even just a "bad hair day," we can suggest a discipline program for it that might work. The key is to be tough but fair to the hair. *(That rhymes!)* One way to solve the "bad hair" problem is just to stuff it all in a headband or hat. Another solution for bad hair is to put your hair up in a loose or "messy" bun with a hair band. But don't be tempted to cut it all off . . . you may regret that decision later!

★ *MYTHICAL BAD HAIR:* Medusa (the character from Greek mythology) had snakes for hair, so imagine what her hair looked like when they were digesting mice! And when it came time for the snakes to shed their skin, well . . . that was "hat day."

Hair Frequently Asked Questions (FAQs)

WHY ARE SOME HAIRS STRAIGHT, WHILE OTHERS ARE CURLY?

A hair grows out of a root in your skin called a *follicle.* If the shape of the hair shaft at its root is *round,* the hair is *straight.* If the shaft is *flattened,* the hair will be *curly.* And if the shaft is *oval,* the hair will be *wavy.*

WHAT DECIDES THE COLOR OF MY HAIR?

You have a color or "pigment" in your body called *melanin.* This coloring is in your eyes, your skin, and in your hair follicles. Whatever color melanin you inherited from your ancestors is what you get for your hair color. (Unless you use dye!)

WHY DOES HAIR TURN GRAY OR WHITE AS A PERSON GETS OLDER?

Your body makes less melanin as you get older. So where there used to be a *color* in the hair, an older hair has *air bubbles* instead. Strange, huh? Air bubbles *in* the hair. These air bubbles are what make an older person's hair look gray and white!

IS IT BAD FOR MY HAIR IF I PULL ON IT?

Yes. This nervous habit can damage your hair roots and lead to hair loss. The compulsion to pull on hair is called *trichotillomania,* and nine times as many women as men have it.

WHY DON'T GIRLS GET BEARDS?

Because that would look bad.

Washing Your Hair

Hair experts agree that you don't need to automatically shampoo your hair every day! It sounds weird, but your hair looks healthier if there's a little natural oil in it, so why waste all that water?

★ The strangest shampoo we've heard of is Grenade Shampoo. This was a hair care product that came in a grenade-shaped bottle. To get the shampoo to come out, you had to pull a pin!

If you want your hair shiny and aromatic, eucalyptus trees make an oil that can give your scalp a nice tingle and a fresh forest smell. After washing your hair, get some eucalyptus oil and rub it into your hair to see if you like it.

★ A salon in England started using "caviar conditioner" in 2005. (Caviar is a food made from fish eggs.) For about $350, a person gets to have fish eggs stuck in their hair. The fish oil is supposed to be good for it.

Speaking of organic hair treatments, here are two that you may want to try.

Go Heavy on the Mayo!

Your own all-natural conditioner!

YOU WILL NEED: Mayonnaise, a plastic bag or towel.

If you're trying to give your hair some life, there are girls who swear by their mayonnaise bottles. Just go ahead and shampoo your hair like normal, and then fill your palms with globs of mayonnaise and work it into your hair!

Once you have it pretty well mayo'ed, cover your hair with a plastic bag or towel for about 15 minutes. Then wash it out. We can *almost* guarantee that your hair won't be dull after doing this.

★ Note: Mustard doesn't work as a conditioner. (You'll end up smelling like Grey Poupon.)

Split End Serum

If your hair's too dry, olives are the answer!

YOU WILL NEED: Olive oil, a damp towel or shower cap.

Warm up ¼ cup of olive oil a little bit in the microwave and then work it into your hair. Once it's been massaged in, wrap a warm, damp towel around your head (or use a shower cap) and leave it on for 15 minutes or so. Then take off the towel or cap and shampoo.

Then shampoo again! If your hair doesn't come out moisturized and luxuriant, you can have your money back. If you do this once a week, it will really start to show.

Drying Your Hair

Ready to dry your hair? Use a towel! Either that or set your blow-dryer to a low setting. That's because Dr. Janet

A Little Syrup on the Side ☺

A sweet shampoo prank for a loved one near you!

You will need: Pancake syrup

What with all the organic shampoos available, why not treat a family member to a shampoo of your own invention? Once a shampoo bottle has been finished, snag it from the recycling and fill it up partway with pancake syrup. If you think your potential victim will be fairly clueless, put the old bottle (with the syrup) back in the shower and remove the new bottle. If your victim is more observant, wait until their "real" shampoo bottle reaches the level of your syrup bottle . . . then switch them.

We're not waffling when we say that there will be loads of laughs from this one! (And don't worry, the pancake syrup washes right out.)

Roberts (professor of dermatology and hair loss expert) says: "Blow-drying with a hot hair dryer is the most damaging thing that women do on a daily basis [to their hair]."

Hair Styling

Like we said, your hair goes up and stays in place better if it isn't *perfectly clean.* Your hair's natural oils are sort of your own styling gel. You've seen women (and men) with hair that is "grungy" or messed-up on purpose. How stylish! The thing is, you just know that these people didn't actually stop washing their hair. Maybe they use a product like "Rusk." Rusk was a hair styling product that gave clean hair "the look and feel of hair that hadn't been washed for days." Really!

If you ever want to really spike your hair up, use the punk rock recipe: *Egg whites!* Crack a bunch of eggs, separate the yolks from the whites, and start working the egg whites into your hair. What a mess!

But it will dry and stiffen into beautiful spikes.

★ *CURLING IRON JUSTICE!* In Shreveport, Louisiana, a man entered a beauty college to rob it. The store's manager yelled, "Get that sucker!" as the man tried to leave. He was arrested after the students and teachers attacked him with curling irons.

Maybe now you're ready to do some braiding! The "rule of thumb" to do this is that your hair be long enough to fall past your shoulders. And it's easier and more fun to braid your friend's hair and then have her braid yours.

We're sure you've done this before, but . . . all you have to do is get your hair into a ponytail and then put a tie around it. Separate the hair into three parts. Then start braiding by bringing the right part over the center part. Then bring the left part over the new center. Keep doing that! Tie it off at the end with elastic.

Hey, besides braids, do you already use one of these hairstyles?

BRaid   FRench bRaid   tWists   buns

ponytail   CORNROWS   pigtails

These are all styles that can **pull** on your hair for long periods of time. Believe it or not, over time, this can all lead to some form of **baldness.** If there is too much tension on your hair, you will start noticing broken strands. From there, your hair may start getting shorter and thinner. The scientific term for this is **traction alopecia.** What it means is that the hair falls out and doesn't come back. (So be sure to give your hair a rest from these styles sometimes.)

Nurses, people from India, and African Americans are *most* likely to get this condition. The same thing can happen when tight curlers are being used. Hot combing, chemical straighteners, and "hair relaxing" have also been found to sometimes cause thin hair.

★ About 20 percent of women will experience some hair loss in their lives. Men suffer from a 50 percent baldness rate.

To take care of your hair, avoid using harsh chemicals on it. Be sure to eat some protein during the day (since that's what your hair is made of), use gentle shampoos, and don't brush too much. A pick or comb with wide teeth does the least amount of damage to hair.

Haircuts and Coloring

"READ LOTS OF BOOKS SO YOU DON'T END UP WITH A $75 HAIRCUT SITTING ON A $10 BRAIN." —Rose Leaf

No matter how much you love your hairstyle now, in 10 years you will look at pictures of yourself and be embarrassed. *It's the law of fashion.* Then 10 years after that, your pictures will look good again! Anyway, you've probably had your hair cut in a salon. The average cost for a "salon" haircut is around $20 to $30. If the salon has more than 13 chairs, it will run you closer to $50. Big-shot hairdressers in New York can charge as much as $800 for a haircut! Let's see, assuming that the haircut takes 80 minutes, that would be $10 a *minute* . . . Heck, just to have the hairdresser look at your hair for a second would cost a dollar!

★ *THINK OF THE MONEY THEY SAVE!* There is a tribe of people who live on Madagascar named the Tsimihety. Their name translates to "the people who don't cut their hair."

If your haircutter is someone you trust, and she wants to try something a little different with your hair, that's okay. But be stern with your haircutter if she just wants to do "*her* thing" with your hair. If you do ever get a bad haircut, the last thing you want to hear is "Don't worry, it'll grow out." You want it to look better *now!*

How to Deal with a Bad Haircut

Rearrange it with barrettes!

Hide it with a cute hat!

OR try to grow it out fast!

Natural Auburn Highlights

"Auburn" is a brownish-red color that looks good in almost everyone's hair!

YOU WILL NEED: Henna powder (henna is a plant with leaves that are perfect for skin and hair dyes).

Put ¼ cup of henna in a plastic cup and bring it in the shower with you. Get your hair wet, and then divert some hot water into the cup of henna. Mix it around with your finger. Once it's well mixed, pour it on your head.

Work the henna around in your hair and then go about your usual shower routine, keeping your head away from the water. When you're ready to condition and/or shampoo, just wash out the henna and do your regular thing. You will have lovely auburn highlights when you get out of the shower.

Natural Blonde Highlights

How to get natural highlights that aren't naturally yours!

YOU WILL NEED: A lemon, some salt, a sunny day.

If you want to keep it organic, here's the way to highlight your hair. Squeeze a lemon into a bowl until all the juice is gone. Add a teaspoon of salt and stir it up.

Then lean your head over a sink and work the concoction into your hair. Rub it in well; then go outside. Let your hair sit in full sunlight for a couple of hours. Then go back inside, rinse your hair with some water, and dry it. ***Ta-dah!***

★ Celtic fashion! You'd probably rather not style your hair the way the ancient Celts of Europe did. They soaked their hair with a mixture of water and crushed chalk, which made the hairs stick up in pale, stiff clumps. The hair spikes were so stiff that you could impale an apple on one!

Body Hair

Not all women shave. As a matter of fact, the whole *idea* of shaving body hair is a very recent development. Most cultures haven't worried much about hair on a girl's body. And in the United States, women never showed their armpits or bare legs in public, so some hair in the armpits or on the legs was no big deal.

★ There are even places in Asia where a slight mustache on a woman was seen as attractive!

So why the change? *Fashion.* Blouses without sleeves became popular in 1915, and dresses that showed a woman's leg soon followed. **How shocking!** The old rule of "If you don't show it, don't worry about it" had to be changed. And then nylons came out, and they are uncomfortable to wear with hairy legs. Razor companies saw their chance to advertise to women for the first time, and nothing's been the same since.

These days, some girls shave because they've seen their mothers shave and it seems "adult." Girls with light skin and dark body hair might shave because body hair can be seen more easily on them. Many black girls (and of course, many women of all races) don't shave at all.

★ Thirty percent of men between the ages of 18 to 34 shave their chests.

Good Shaving Tips

1. CHECK WITH YOUR MOM BEFORE SHAVING. ONCE YOU START SHAVING, YOU CAN STOP ANYTIME, BUT YOU PROBABLY WON'T!

2. BATHING BEFOREHAND WILL PREPARE YOUR SKIN AND SOFTEN THE HAIRS. AND USE SHAVING CREAM!

3. DON'T PUSH THE RAZOR DOWN HARD. RAZORS

ARE RAZOR-SHARP, AND THEY DON'T NEED MUCH PRESSURE TO WORK!

4. TRY TO SHAVE WITHOUT TURNING THE RAZOR SIDEWAYS. (NOTHING IS WORSE THAN GETTING A NICK IN THE UNDERARM OR ON YOUR ANKLE!)

5. DON'T USE A DULL RAZOR!

252

6. BE CAREFUL!

There are other ways to deal with unwanted hair. For instance, *electrolysis* involves electrocuting the root of a hair to kill it. (It hurts.) **Laser hair removal** is a more recent version of the same idea. It costs about $1,200 for a full treatment. (It hurts, too.) A famous hair removal technique is the **hot wax treatment.** The idea of this is to pour hot lava—we mean, hot *wax*—onto an area where hair is not wanted. The wax then cools and is then pulled off, sort of like a big Band-Aid. **Wax on, wax off!** Does it hurt? Of course it hurts!

Shopping

Think about money. Everyone knows that a $100 bill is worth a hundred times more than a $1 bill. *But why?* The two bills are the same size, shape, and color. It just so happens that one of them has a different number in the corner. *That's the only difference!*

Money is a game of make-believe. We all *pretend* that money is actually worth something. We put different numbers in the corners of pieces of paper to show how much they're worth. *So what!* We take our little pieces of paper (cash) or plastic (credit or debit cards) and act like they are actually worth something. But it's really just *paper* and *plastic*. The only value they have is in our minds.

But even though it's only make-believe, people devote a lot of time to money. Earning it, saving it, spending it, watching it, and worrying about it . . . many adults spend most of their time dealing with money! Have they forgotten it's not real? When adults get *too* caught up in money, this is what's called the *Rat Race*. (And the only ones who win that race are rats!)

Shopping

Girls love to shop! You're already good at it, but now it's time to get better.

Fun Ca$h Fact$!

$$ The first coin ever designed in the United States said "Mind Your Business" on it. Benjamin Franklin came up with the idea.

$$ The "$" sign originally had two vertical lines running through the S. The two vertical lines represented a U superimposed over the S, which stood for U.S., the United States. Over time, the U lost its bottom and then lost one of its lines. The United States is the only country that used its own name on its money symbol. Today, the symbol means "money" all over the world.

$$ It costs about two cents to make, print, and cut a dollar bill. Guess how much it costs to print a $100 bill? About two cents!

$$ *SECRET INFORMATION!* Look carefully in the top right corner of a $1 dollar bill. If you stare hard enough, you will see the little owl who lives up there.

Shop Smart

Girls usually spend most of their money on clothing, shoes, accessories, cosmetics, knickknacks, and high-tech items (such as cell phones or iPods). So how can you be a smart shopper and make sure not to waste your money?

You Don't Want to Hear This!

A survey of mall shoppers found that the most annoying thing a sales clerk can say is "That's not my department." Other most-hated phrases included "If it's not on the rack, we don't have it," "I'm on a break," "The computer is down," "Sorry, this is my first day," and "I don't work here."

ASK YOURSELF THESE QUESTIONS:

1. *WHY DO YOU WANT IT?* Shopping is not always logical. Sometimes you just want something *because* you want

it. But can you figure out why you want it? Is it really cool, or is it just because everyone else has it?

2. *IF YOU WANT TO BUY SOMETHING, CAN YOU MAKE YOURSELF WAIT A LITTLE?* Try leaving the store, and then shop around to make sure there's not a better deal at another store. (This also will help you decide if you really want something.)

3. *DOES THE ITEM YOU WANT SEEM LIKE IT'S AT A FAIR PRICE?* Stores won't necessarily charge you a *fair* price. They will charge the amount people are *willing to pay*. This is called "charging what the market will bear." Name-brand items and "in" products usually cost more, because stores can get away with charging more.

Let's say that you want a new shirt. If you buy it new at a store, you are probably paying *twice* as much as the store paid the shirt maker. And if you're buying jewelry, the store's markup is even worse! So is it a rip-off? (As long as you're wondering about this, you're a step ahead of most people.)

★ *THEY'RE WATCHING YOU!* By charting where girls shop inside of stores, researchers have learned that girls spend most of their time on the right side of the stores they go into.

★ *THE BUSIEST SHOPPING DAYS OF THE YEAR!* The two weekends before December 25th are the busiest shopping days of the year. The day after Thanksgiving is the *fifth* most popular.

If you do some comparison shopping online, you can probably find the best deals. Even with shipping costs, you may choose to have an item mailed to your house, because it's cheaper AND it saves you a trip to the store. And if you really want to save money . . .

Go Thrifting

Be smart about spending a little; after all, who said style has to be expensive?

YOU WILL NEED: A desire to save money and to have a good time.

Where can you buy a skirt, tank top, belt, blazer, and silk blouse for just $20? Try your local Salvation Army or Goodwill stores. If you want to be a smart

consumer or just want to find a killer deal, your local thrift shop is the place to do it. Of course, there's a lot of stuff there that's "junky," but just think of it as a treasure hunt!

"Vintage" clothes definitely have character, and they set you apart from everyone else. Plus, there's nothing like bragging about the name-brand "find" you scored for $10!

When you go thrifting, you'll know you're not getting ripped off, and we bet you have a lot of fun. BTW, it's fine to *shop* cheap, but be careful about buying tube tops, small miniskirts, or short-shorts. *Looking cheap* is never cool!

★ *THRIFT SHOPS ARE GREAT PLACES TO FIND HALLOWEEN COSTUMES.*

Clothes

If you find a pair of pants or a sweater (or whatever) in a style you really like

261

and that looks good on you, buy more than one. Get it in different colors or patterns, because if it's a winner, it's a *winner!* Focus on clothes that highlight your strong points. Once you know what looks good on you *and* what you like, you're all set.

Be sure to check the "washing instructions" on the label of any clothes you're thinking about buying. (And to leave the tag on any clothes you buy until you're sure that they fit the way you want them to.) If an item needs dry cleaning, you might want to think twice about buying it. Dry cleaning is sort of a hassle and it can be expensive.

★ *HOT TIP!* If you're thinking about buying something, try to think of three pieces of clothing you already own that could go with-it. If you can't think of three, you might want to pass on it.

★ *IF YOU FEEL LIKE BEING A SPAZZ,* go into a clothing store's fitting room and sing out loudly, "I see London, I see France!"

Shoes

This may seem like obvious advice, but make sure to get shoes that fit! About half of all women are wearing shoes that are TOO SMALL for them.

Try on shoes late in the day, because (believe it or not!) your feet widen as you walk around, so they actually get bigger. Also, the odds are that one of your feet is bigger than the other one, so have your feet carefully measured and then always try the shoes on *both* feet.

★ *NEWS FLASH!* Most men and boys don't *ever* look at anyone's feet, and they don't care how big a girl's shoes are.

If you are planning to actually *walk* much in your new shoes, the heels shouldn't be

Buy It on Sale!

If you've ever made a special trip to a store only to find the place closed, you know that *timing is important*. To have the right timing on some great sales, shop sometime between the middle of January through the start of February. This is when a lot of stores put leftover items from the holiday season up for grabs at good prices.

more than an inch high. And remember that shoes with heels should be almost as cushy and comfy as sports shoes. If they're not, don't buy them!

Cosmetics

Many companies that sell makeup price their products way too high, and they know it. This sounds crazy, but their sales are better when they *overprice* the makeup! Helena Rubenstein made millions of dollars in the makeup business, and she said, "Some women won't buy anything unless they can pay a lot."

In other words, the makeup is so expensive it somehow makes it seem worth it. *Reverse psychology!* How dumb is that?

High-Tech

YOU'RE THE EXPERT. Your parents may not even have had phones when they were growing up, and if they had computers, it was something like an abacus with an

265

electric plug. A ***portable music device*** was a kazoo, not an iPod. Since you are probably more of an expert on electronic gadgets than most adults, use your wisdom wisely.

★ *ARE YOUR EYES SENSITIVE?* Teenage girls buy twice as many sunglasses as boys do. (Maybe this is because sunglasses make your eyes seem big, and they help you hide from the paparazzi.)

Wacky Product Warnings

It's good that companies include safety information with their products. But some companies are so worried about safety (and getting sued), that their product warnings can get a little ridiculous. A group called Michigan Lawsuit Abuse Watch has a contest to find the nation's "wackiest" directions. Read the product warnings on the next pages and ask yourself: Is the company incredibly stupid or do they think we are? All the warnings are taken from real products!

ON A FOLDING BABY STROLLER: "Remove child before folding."

ON A TOILET BRUSH: "Do not use for personal hygiene."

ON A TV REMOTE CONTROL: "Not dishwasher safe."

ON A SCOOTER: "This product moves when used."

ON A CD PLAYER: "Warning—dangerous warning inside."

ON A THERMOMETER USED TO TAKE A PERSON'S TEMPERATURE: "Once used rectally, the thermometer should not be used orally."

ON A WHEELBARROW: "Not intended for highway use."

ON A BLENDER: "Never remove food or other items from the blades while the product is operating."

ON A NINE-BY-THREE-INCH PLASTIC BAG OF AIR USED FOR PACKING: "Do not use this product as a toy, pillow, or flotation device."

ON A ROBOTIC MASSAGE CHAIR: "Do not use massage chair without clothing . . . and, never force any body part into the backrest area while the rollers are moving."

ON A SNOWBLOWER: "Do not use snowblower on roof."

ON A DISHWASHER: "Do not allow children to play in the dishwasher."

ON A THREE-PRONGED FISHHOOK: "Harmful if swallowed."

ON A BOTTLE OF DRAIN CLEANER: "If you do not understand, or cannot read, all directions, cautions, and warnings, do not use this product."

ON A SMOKE DETECTOR: "Do not use the Silence Feature in emergency situations. It will not extinguish a fire."

ON A CAN OF PEPPER SPRAY: "May irritate eyes."

Top Secret Shopping Info!

Only use the following advice if you *really, really, really* need something when you are out shopping with one or both of your parents. (This will probably work better with your dad.)

Here's the situation. ***You see something that you want. A solar-powered sundress?*** I must have it! You know if you just ASK for the dress, you will probably get "No" for an answer. Try hanging out near the item you want and start a conversation like this. (Try to look very wistful and pitiful while you speak.)

YOU: DAD, DO YOU EVER GET SAD THINKING OF ALL THE LONELY PEOPLE?

YOUR DAD: WHY ARE YOU WORRYING ABOUT THAT, HONEY?

YOU: I DON'T KNOW. I JUST LOOK AROUND SOMETIMES AND THINK ABOUT HOW UNFAIR LIFE IS.

DAD: WOW, MY DAUGHTER SURE IS A THOUGHTFUL PERSON.

YOU: NOT REALLY. I JUST WONDER WHY SOME PEOPLE HAVE SUCH SAD LIVES. (LOOK VERY SORROWFUL NOW.)

DAD: TAKE IT EASY! YOU NEED TO CHEER UP!

YOU: I GUESS SO. (YOU GIVE A WEAK SMILE.) SAY, THIS SOLAR-POWERED SUNDRESS IS SORT OF CUTE.

DAD (REACHING FOR HIS CREDIT CARD): IT'S YOURS!

Obviously, this is not a strategy you should use a lot, because it is *wrong*. So just try it once a year! ☺

ACKNOWLEDGMENTS

Sincere thanks to the five King sisters, Pat and Cindy King, Mariam Kanso, Allyson Scharpf, Miranda Schwabauer, Alex Fus, Rachael Mejia, Allison Moore, Megan McKittrick, Kylie Nomi, Kim Fouse, Sarah Wilson, Amanda Lapato, Rebecca Pankow, Sophie Moshofsky, Jessica Hooper, Kelcey Van Orman, Amy Schick, Kristina Chou, Shannon Twomey, Rachel Hahn, and the Lundys.

An earnest shout-out to Janet King, Virginia Wassink, Carlye Krohn, Kathryn Fitch, Amy vanderSommen, Betsy Ray, Laura and Marilyn Erkeneff, Daniel Fredgant, Tyler Kelly, Genevieve Smith, the Harkers, the Zehners, the Wassinks, Deb Hartman, Tammi Vincik, Ron Martin, Kathy Logan, Carolyn Wood, Peggy Brandt, Anne Stevenson, Lynn Schukart, Nadine Chauncey, Rick Kristoff, Janice Johnson, JoAnn Thomas, the Levins, Linda Hall, Patti Larson, Tona Hattery, Leslie Redman, Debbie DuMez, Karen Hughes, Robin Squire, Debbie Groves, Marsha Goldwasser, Karen Youngs, Lisa Sacconaghi, Kristin Heintz, Kim Woodberry, Lainie and Katie King, and Lisa Senter. Also, our sincere thanks to the Multnomah County Library staff.

While we're on the topic, many girls (and boys) use *whining* on their parents to get them to buy "stuff." We hope you know whining is unworthy of you. It's so lame and babyish! However, if you calmly give evidence as to why you should have an item, you are not *whining*. You are making a *reasonable suggestion*.

For a list of this book's sources visit http://www.bartking.net